D0106689

ADVANCE PRAISE FOR *LEAD LIKE YOU WERE MEANT TO*

"Now more than ever, today's business environment requires leaders who are intentional and authentic. Rob McKinnon is the Tesla of executive coaches. His book, *Lead Like You Were Meant To*, helps leaders disrupt their own status quo, master self-awareness, and inspire their organizations. A must-read for all leaders."
—David J Adelman, CEO, Campus Apartments, Darco Capital

"McKinnon's unique four-dimensional framework leads you through a process of self-discovery that helps illuminate your personal barriers and effectively unleash your highest potential. Whether you're just entering the workforce or hold a top-ranking position at your company, this is a must-read for any leader aspiring to advance in their career."
—Berta Aldrich, Managing Director, Private Advisor Group

"Wow . . . unlike other leadership books, Rob McKinnon brilliantly integrates the concepts of leadership growth with engaging examples and pragmatic strategies. In *Lead Like You Were Meant To*, McKinnon nails the real barriers to great leadership and provides a practical guide to overcoming them. An essential read for anyone who wants to expand their leadership capacity and increase their impact."
—Kristin Colber-Baker, Global Head,
Talent Development, Mars, Inc.

"As a Chief Learning Officer, I always look for the best resources to help leaders grow their leadership. In *Lead Like You Were Meant To*, Rob McKinnon provides a very practical guide, using a holistic approach I highly endorse. Beginning with identifying leaders' built-in roadblocks to growth, McKinnon shows the way for leaders to become more aware, measure how they lead, and develop an action plan for long term sustainability. This book is a must read for any leader interested in growing and becoming the best leader he or she can be."

—Al Cornish, Chief Learning Officer, Closing the Gap

"Prepare yourself! Rob McKinnon challenges you to know, understand, and manage your inner self so you can lead effectively on the outside. Consider this book the *Blink* of leadership—enhanced preparation for high-stakes decision-making and problem-solving. *Lead Like You Were Meant To* provides a path with clear steps to reach your highest self-awareness, discover your own full potential, and bring out the best in others."

—John Darby, CEO, The Beach Company

"Leaders Need Not Read This Book. Leaders Need To LIVE This Book!"

—Kenny Dichter, CEO, Wheels Up

"Every leader should read this book, right now. *Lead Like You Were Meant To* is exactly what leaders need in the age of Covid . . . or any time! The exhausting schedule of one video call after another all day long makes it easier than ever to go on autopilot and just try to get through the day. This book got me refocused on my purpose, which gets me out of autopilot and into awareness—awareness of who I am, the kind of leader I want to be, and the legacy I want to leave."

—Ron Farmer, COO, Fullsteam

"My senior colleagues and I have benefited from Rob's coaching for many years. He's helped us grow personally and professionally and understand ourselves and each other. In business, he's a competitive advantage. In life, he's a trusted advisor and friend. We're all so excited to share his approach and methods with our friends and colleagues now that he's written a book that includes his teachings. It's a fun read—the illustrations are great, and the anecdotes are quite instructive."

—Michael Forman, Chairman and CEO, FS Investments

"In *Lead Like You Were Meant To*, leaders now have a thoughtful, thorough, and relatable guide to enhance their self-awareness, be fully present in all interactions, and become the truly authentic leader they were meant to be."

—Dr. William A. Gentry, Author of the best-selling book *Be the Boss Everyone Wants to Work For: A Guide for New Leaders*

"*Lead Like You Were Meant To* is not only a refreshing new way to approach growing as a leader, it is potentially liberating . . . even life-changing! Reading it will help you lead better, and live better—with lighter burdens, greater impact, and more joy. Combining deep knowledge of both leadership and what it takes to thrive as a human being, Rob McKinnon has offered leaders and their organizations a great gift with this book."

—Reverend Bill Haley, Executive Director, Coracle

"Rob was my coach for over ten years until the successful sale of my company. He is the best! I applied the principles he lays out in *Lead Like You Were Meant To*, and they helped me immensely—professionally and personally. Read this book if you want to grow as a leader. And hire Rob if you want the full experience!"

—John Lynch, Retired CEO & President,
Educational Computer Systems, Inc. (ECSI)

"They say people don't come with instruction manuals. Well, now they do."

—Joel McGlamry, CEO, Hennessy Automobile Companies

"Keep this leadership book close at hand. Rob McKinnon will speak to you as he spoke to me on leadership dimensions that you likely have not considered. Effective leaders must continue to grow. Get ready to up your game with this book. As a student of leadership in war, peace, and now the boardroom, I suggest you invite Rob to be your leadership coach and mentor in *Lead Like You Were Meant To*."

—Joseph Rank, Vice President and Chief Executive, Lockheed Martin Saudi Arabia, Brigadier General (retired), U.S. Army

"Awesome read . . . different from any other book on leadership! *Lead Like You Were Meant To* will poignantly remind you WHY you became a leader! Rob McKinnon provides the essential, practical tools for being the very best version of yourself—to be well and to lead well. And it is a must read for any leader who is intentional about developing those they lead."

—Cindi Roth, President & CEO, West Virginia University Foundation

"*Lead Like You Were Meant To* is the perfect book for leaders to read again and again. It made me think, smile, reflect, and promise myself I can keep getting better. I expect to consult this book and Rob's suggestions often. It has helped increase my self-awareness and, in turn, my self-leadership so that I show up for meetings (or Zoom calls!) prepared to lead well with 100% of myself."

—JM Schapiro, CEO, Continental Realty Corporation

"This is a must read for any leader, in any industry. Rob's coaching not only transformed the way I lead at work, but also changed how I show up with family and friends—making me better in all areas of my life. Somehow, Rob distilled the magic of his one-on-one coaching into a deep, engaging, and powerful book that will help you live and lead as the very best version of yourself."

—Rabbi Mike Uram, Author of *Next Generation Judaism* and Campus Rabbi, University of Pennsylvania

"Rob McKinnon's book is an absolute treasure and powerhouse resource for coaches . . . and the leaders they coach! He provides clear, concise methods to bring deep universal concepts to leaders for the sake of helping them create more powerful connection, internally and externally. Coaches—who recognize that leadership is an inside game—will find exercises, roadmaps, charts, takeaways, and reflection questions that are perfectly on point for lasting leadership transformation."

—Christine Wahl, M.A.Ed., MCC, and Founder, Georgetown University Leadership Coaching Program

"Love this book. McKinnon does a masterful job of weaving together a leader's four dimensions and how they combine for leadership presence, self-management, and execution. I often found myself as a character in his useful stories. *Lead Like You Were Meant To* will challenge you to examine your default modes (and which ones you want to change!) as you become more aware, assess, and adjust your leadership."

—Steve Wilhite, SVP, Schneider Electric; Former CEO, Summit Energy

"Rob's book helps me take an often-needed inward pause, and use the four dimensions framework to address my own leadership challenges and opportunities. That pause, and the work around the physical, intellectual, emotional, and spiritual dimensions, enables me to step out as a more balanced leader, and lead with better internal awareness, grace, and strength. Thanks Rob, for sharing this great tool with me and others!"

—Yasser Youssef, President, The Budd Group

LEAD

LIKE YOU
WERE
MEANT TO

Make the Switch from
Autopilot to Intentional

ROB McKINNON

IVEY
BOOKS

Published by Ivey Books

GIRL FRIDAY
PRODUCTIONS®
Edited and designed by Girl Friday Productions
www.girlfridayproductions.com
Design: Paul Barrett
Project management: Alexander Rigby
Image credits: cover © Shutterstock/greenmax

ISBN (hardcover): 978-1-7350850-0-5
ISBN (paperback): 978-1-7350850-1-2
ISBN (ebook): 978-1-7350850-2-9

To Marta—
Strong, beautiful woman.
Love of my life.
Faithful companion in the journey.

CONTENTS

PREFACE

I have discovered that one of the most interesting challenges in writing this book was deciding on the title. Which few words do you choose to capture the attention of busy leaders, and at the same time give them a clue as to what the book is about?! As my marketing friend Terry says, "The headline is 80% of the story!"

Ever since Marta and I moved to Charlottesville, one of my favorite activities is my daily fitness workout at Keswick Hall with our trainer Tracey. I show up for an hour every morning and just surrender to her program. She brings variety, motivation and relentless challenge that encourages me to do more. Under her coaching, other than when I was a young Army officer, I'm probably in the best shape of my life.

Tracey provides a plan, and she will push. But she gives room for you to work according to your own ability, your own fitness goals. If I "complain" about the amount of weight or if I want to do a higher number of reps, I will hear back from her, "You do you!"

In the same way, this book provides a plan, and is intended to push you, with the intent that "You do you!" Except, for leaders, I say, "Lead Like You!"

You should find this to be a different kind of leadership book. Rather than chapter after chapter telling you how to be like someone else, this book is intended to help you lead more out of the best version of who you are—to *Lead Like You Were Meant To*. But, and this is where the sub-title comes in, you will have to 'make the switch,' turn off awareness-numbing 'autopilot,' and lead yourself more intentionally.

So there you are. If you've read this far, something prompted you to pick up the book. Hopefully, the title helped!

Lead well.

Rob McKinnon
Keswick, Virginia
July 2020

GET READY TO LEAD LIKE YOU WERE MEANT TO

I stepped into the elevator and pressed the top button on the panel—the sixty-fifth floor. The doors closed, and we began our ascent. The elevator car was full, and there were many stops along the way. But somewhere around the sixtieth floor, the elevator emptied out, and I rode the last leg alone to the top.

When the doors opened, I was greeted by a security guard in a small white-marble vestibule. I gave him my name and then stood there, waiting. After about five minutes, Susan stepped through the tall double doors and escorted me back. We passed no one as we made our trip to the large corner office of the leader I was going to meet for the first time.

I would later learn that only the CEO, the COO, and the general counsel, along with their executive assistants, occupied the top floor of this massive building. Seven people, including the security guard. Other than rides in the elevator, it was conceivable that each of these senior leaders could go a whole day and not see another person.

In a very palpable way, I was reminded that day that few leaders get to the very top. And for those who do get there, the journey can be an increasingly isolating one. Even if they work in an open, bustling office with lots of coworkers and plenty of interaction, when it comes to their biggest challenges or decisions—the ones that come with their leadership roles— they might as well be alone on the sixty-fifth floor.

I had been introduced to Steve, the president and COO of the company, through his doctor, of all people. During a routine annual exam, Steve had complained about how much stress he was experiencing at work, and his doctor, observing the toll it was taking, was at a loss to help him. So the doctor suggested Steve talk to me.

As I entered Steve's large corner office with its floor-to-high-ceiling windows overlooking the city, I found the usual array of executive accessories: family pictures; a few awards and keepsakes; evidence of his golf, fishing, and hunting hobbies; and several shelves of top leadership books from the past couple of decades.

Steve clearly knew how to lead. And he had all the technical skills needed to be COO of this large Fortune 500 company. But as we sat down together in his comfortable seating area, I learned that Steve had finally run into a leadership problem that all his experience and all the books on his shelf provided no help with.

He had a good working relationship with his boss, the CEO. Together they had led the company to grow significantly over the past five years. But occasionally the boss would say and do things that led Steve to think his boss didn't have complete confidence in him. Steve's thinking and feeling led to him experiencing great stress.

And now, as we had our introductory conversation, I learned that Steve wanted me to coach him to figure out what else his boss needed from him and how to do it. If Steve couldn't get the affirmation he needed from his boss and couldn't find the answer in a book, he would just hire a coach to tell him what to do. I would go on to tell him that's not how I coach. And that wasn't his real problem anyway!

When I meet behind closed doors with leaders and begin to have conversations with them, I hear about some of their biggest challenges, particularly the challenges the company is facing. But, more significantly, I hear frustrations and questions about their own leadership. They sense that they could be doing better. They want to keep growing. Sometimes they know the specific area that needs attention. Other times they just have a general intuition that they could do better. *Lead better.* Their company doesn't necessarily know it, but they know it.

> ## You are a leader. But who is leading you?

HOW DO YOU GET BETTER AS A LEADER?

You are a leader. But who is leading you? Who is helping you be a better leader? You may have a boss or a board that holds you accountable. But who is leading you—all the time?

If you noodle over that a bit, you come to the realization that no one else is leading you all the time. No other person can. Only you are leading you—all the time, in every situation. You are leading yourself. You are holding yourself accountable. You are trying to make yourself better.

Herein lies the hidden trap of success as a leader. As you progress, pass your peers, and move toward the top of your organization, you become more isolated. And as you are becoming more isolated, you are also being challenged to lead in new ways and new areas that you probably have not encountered before. Leaders at the top are at the top because others believe that only they know how to do what needs to be done.

So what do you do if you are one of these leaders and you want to get better? Where do you turn? And where do you find teachers that specialize in the type of learning that you need? Who can you be vulnerable with about your weaknesses? To whom can you admit, "I don't have all the answers and I need help"? The notion "It's lonely at the top" has come to characterize senior leadership for good reason.

The more success you have as a leader, the more isolated you become. And yet, to grow, you must intentionally engage personal development on your own.[1] No one else in your organization has all the answers you are seeking. To be clear, no outsiders have all the answers either. This would include writers, speakers, consultants, gurus, and famous CEOs with their pictures on the front of their books.

> ## You possess everything you need to be a better leader.
> ## You're just not using all of it.

So I tell these leaders who sense something is missing what I will tell you.

You possess everything you need to be a better leader.

You're just not using all of it.

Instead of asking for another list of *things to do*, you need to focus on fully knowing yourself—*and being who you are*. Lead like you were meant to!

My guess is that, if you are like most of the leaders I meet, you're using 60 to maybe 80 percent of your potential. But not

100 percent. That's why you need a new leadership model: to close the gap.

A lot of bad things can happen in the gap—things that undermine, derail, or pollute all the good from the other 60 to 80 percent of your effectiveness. Are you aware of the gap? Are you aware that something is missing?

This book introduces a new framework that will help you know yourself better. Rather than beginning with doing, it enables you to see yourself as a leader in a whole new way. And out of that *seeing* will emerge a new way of *being*. And out of the *being* will emerge new ways of *doing*, new ways of *leading*, from the same leader—*you*! The model I use is the foundation for my life's work, which I describe as "Helping leaders be the *best* version of themselves possible."

I call this leadership framework "four-dimensional leadership," so named because you show up to lead in four dimensions: physically, intellectually, emotionally, and spiritually. Four-dimensional leaders know how to get better and be at their best. They have more influence and are more effective than other leaders for three key reasons:

- **They are more *aware*.** They observe and are aware of their present leadership capabilities and vulnerabilities before others see them (or suffer from them!).

- **They *assess* better.** They know instantaneously what adjustments are needed to close gaps and increase their capacity to lead.

- **They *adjust* better.** They rebalance and strengthen themselves in each of their four dimensions to maximize their leadership influence in the moment.

The notion that leaders (all humans, really) have four dimensions is an ancient one. But after over a decade of coaching leaders of all ages, vocations, and career levels, from college graduates in their first job to veteran CEOs approaching retirement, I have found that, in every case, the application of this four-dimensional leadership framework is new!

HOW DO YOU KNOW IF THIS BOOK IS FOR YOU?

You've picked this book up, but is it really for you? Reading a book is an investment of time. So let me save you some time here at the beginning, because if you're like most of the successful leaders I work with, you don't have a lot of extra time. Even though they have all the business bestsellers on their office bookshelves, many leaders don't take the time to read for personal development. And even those who do read have little time to read a whole book.

If you fit into any of the following situations, just know I wrote this book for you.

Situation 1: You Are a Leader Who Simply Wants to Grow

Many of the leaders I work with are already doing pretty well before I come along. They have no glaring deficits or problems as leaders. In fact, most of them have accumulated a track record of success. They lead large companies or divisions with thousands of people impacted by their leadership. Many have already become multimillionaires as a result of their success—a few even billionaires.

I'm always curious, then, about these accomplished leaders' interest in coaching. Aren't they already doing everything right? Haven't they already proven to themselves and to the world that they have what it takes to be a leader?

What I've discovered is that most of them are simply demonstrating why they are a good leader: great leaders want to keep growing!

If you want your company, your business unit, or your team to grow, you, as a leader, must grow. If you want different and better outcomes tomorrow, you must lead differently than the way you were leading yesterday.

Great leaders want to keep growing!

This book will help you grow and lead with greater capacity and presence.

Situation 2: You Are a Leader Who Has Had a Setback

Leaders have setbacks. The best ones make a choice to grow from the setbacks and become even better leaders.

Perhaps you've gotten a negative review by your boss, you've been passed over for promotion, or you've even been fired. Whatever it was, you never saw it coming. Or you knew how you needed to change but just couldn't make the switch quickly enough.

Well, let me give you some good news. You are actually in a great place—a great place to learn!

For the first time, you realize what has gotten you this far won't be enough to take you to the next milestone. To use a phrase that has become a bit of a cliché in business coaching (but is still full of wisdom), "What got you here won't get you there."[2]

Growing leaders learn the most in the crucible of personal challenge or pain. They learn more about who they are and what they're missing. They are awakened out of their day-to-day leadership trance. Suddenly, they see themselves and the world around them with new eyes. They begin to ask new questions. Why didn't I get that promotion? Why is my boss or my board upset with me? What is it I'm not seeing? And they begin to look within themselves for answers instead of blaming others.

> Growing leaders learn the most in the crucible of personal challenge or pain.

If you've had a setback, this book will help you see new aspects of yourself—new opportunities to show up differently and lead more effectively.

Situation 3: You Are a Leader Who Wants to Leave a Legacy

Maybe you aspire to do more than just your duty and collect your paycheck. (This notion tends to come to certain leaders after they've been doing their duty and collecting their paychecks for a while. So if you're in your twenties or thirties and this is a foreign notion, don't sweat it.) You've put in a lot of years as a leader and gotten pretty good at what you do. You execute on all the assignments given to you and your team. Your responsibilities have grown, and so have your results. You may feel you are near or at the top of your game as a leader.

But you want more. You want to impact lives. You have your own leadership heroes, but now you want to be someone else's hero. You want to leave a legacy.

Great leaders leave behind a legacy of great leaders.

One successful leader I know wanted to use his influence to positively impact the city where he grew up and improve race relations. Another, a company founder who was ready to retire, wanted to successfully transition the company leadership to his children. Yet another wanted to donate not only a significant portion of his wealth but also his leadership know-how to high-impact community-service organizations.

> ## Great leaders leave behind a legacy of great leaders.

If you are a leader in this territory, wanting to impact the lives of others, you must lead with more than just your brains or your brawn. If you want to engage the hearts and souls of others, you must do so with your own heart and soul.

This book will help you consider your purpose and legacy and lead with all of yourself so you will have the greatest impact on others.

So if any or all of the above situations describe you, you need a new model and new tools to lead yourself better, close the gaps, increase your capacity, and expand your leadership influence. This book provides you with the model and tools to get better as a leader.

WHAT WERE MY GOALS AS I WROTE THIS BOOK FOR YOU?

In order to create as useful a resource as possible for you, I wrote this book with these four intentions in mind:

- **Make it readable.** Most of the leaders I work with have very little time to read. So I have done my best to streamline the essential messages— not bury them under pages of justification or research.

- **Make it rereadable.** The transformational leadership change that this book describes does not happen overnight. You need to practice and practice some more. To support your ongoing practice (and to keep you from needing to reread the whole book multiple times), I have provided chapter summaries and diagrams so you can easily remind yourself of critical concepts.

- **Make it actionable.** I've attempted to write as if I were sitting across from you and having a conversation. Most of the questions are *not* rhetorical— they are intended to help you stop and think. And at the conclusion of each chapter, I have provided questions for reflection to make the book come alive in your day-to-day leadership.

- **Make it a "short-shelf" book.** In my office study, three of the four walls are lined with books. But one shelf, which is easily accessible, is what I call my "short shelf," because it contains a couple dozen books that I consider my essential go-to books on a variety of topics. My hope is that you find this book accessible and a ready reference manual that you keep close at hand and pick up regularly.

WHAT IS THE PATH TO LEADING LIKE YOU WERE MEANT TO?

Lead Like You Were Meant To follows the pattern I use with every leader I coach. When I begin an engagement, I draw the leader a timeline for how we will spend our next six months together (see figure 1). It shouldn't take you six months to read this book, but we will follow the same three steps: be aware, assess, and adjust.

Much as a marksman follows the steps—ready, aim, fire—to increase the chances he will hit his target, leaders need to follow these three steps to increase their impact and effectiveness. When you skip a step, or do them out of order, your results are more likely to be scattered or downright ineffective.

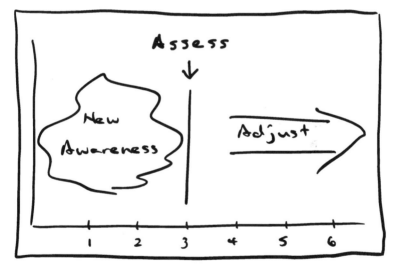

Figure 1. *The McKinnon Way six-month leadership coaching timeline.*

Part 1 is all about becoming aware. In chapter 1, I identify the three most common roadblocks leaders who want to get better face, and the three steps you must take to get past them.

In chapters 2 through 7, we take a deep dive into becoming aware of how you (and every leader) show up to lead in four dimensions: physical, intellectual, emotional, and spiritual. As you read these chapters, you will immediately, naturally, begin changing, growing, and getting better as a leader.

Chapter 8 addresses default patterns that leaders fall into and how these patterns expose the relationship between your greatest strengths and your greatest weaknesses.

Part 2 enables you to build on your newfound awareness and become agile in *assessing* and *adjusting* your leadership, especially when you are under stress and need to lead well. You'll notice that part 2 is relatively short compared to part 1. This reflects the fact that a leader gets better primarily by becoming more aware! But we need to translate the awareness into lasting change, and that is what we address in part 2.

Chapter 9, "Assess," equips you with options to measure how you're leading—whether on your drive in to work, in the middle of a difficult conversation, or when stress pushes you to your wits' end.

Once you know how to better assess yourself, chapter 10 gives you tools to adjust—both in the moment and for lasting change. It concludes with a six-step Personal Action Plan for your own leadership growth. Finally, chapter 11 provides you with examples of real leaders who have successfully applied this four-dimensional framework for transformational change in themselves.

This is the path for how a leader gets better. I know because for fifteen years I have coached all types of leaders who have followed this process. Most of these were CEOs or senior executives. Many were already good leaders who had achieved a lot of success. They ranged in age from their late twenties to seventy-two. Their companies spanned entrepreneurial start-up to middle-market to Fortune 500. All learned to lead themselves and their people better following the steps and framework described in this book.

And you can too. Real growth takes time and is risky and scary. This book will equip you to take the journey with courage and confidence.

So turn the page and get ready to become a better version of yourself. Get ready to lead like you were meant to!

BE AWARE

CHAPTER 1

GETTING PAST THE THREE ROADBLOCKS

If you always do what you've always done,
you'll always get what you always got.
—Commonly attributed to Henry Ford

Generally, the familiar, precisely because it is
familiar, is not known.
—Georg Wilhelm Friedrich Hegel

I once had lunch with a leader who was performing the whole time we were together. I would estimate he did 80 percent of the talking during our ninety minutes together. And I wasn't asking a lot of questions! His face was animated, his eyebrows going up and down repeatedly. He would smile and laugh even when discussing sad events in his life.

As we sat opposite each other in the booth, way in the back of a restaurant so we could have some privacy, I felt as if I were attending a matinee show, where he was up on the stage and I was down in the audience.

He told me about several of his "principles" for living life. He shared "lessons" he had learned and passed on to others.

His stories sounded like they had been delivered many times before. I'm sure I was hearing some of his best material.

He attacked his food and ate it hurriedly, as if time spent swallowing would be a barrier to his talking. He spoke of how important "authenticity" was to him, and yet somehow I never felt like I connected with the part of him that was real. The words he spoke seemed to be words intended to impress me. He didn't seem to feel his feelings. I was wondering how connected he was with his thoughts, his emotions, and his true self. (He reminded me of myself a couple of decades ago!)

And I think this guy is a good leader. For the past six years, he has led one of the most influential organizations in town. You don't stay in a position like that if you are not getting things done. But I wonder how much more impact he could have if he was not playing a role but fully being himself?

THE LEADER'S THREE ROADBLOCKS TO GETTING BETTER

Why is growth as a leader difficult? What is it that keeps all of us from being at our best, or at least from getting better?

I have found in my years of working with leaders that there is not just one but three significant roadblocks to leadership growth. These barriers keep leaders from seeing themselves as they really are. Every leader I know confronts one or more of these roadblocks, including the leaders who, by every measure, seem to have the most success. They hold me back. And I'm sure they are holding you back.

Roadblock 1: Staying in Autopilot

During our lunch conversation, the leader across from me was clearly on autopilot. In ways that are sometimes obvious to you, and in many ways that are not, you operate on autopilot much of the time too. Life happens to you, and you respond, automatically.

The alarm clock goes off, and you get up and begin your morning "routine." Someone who works for you asks you a question, and you have an answer, automatically. An email comes in from your biggest customer, and you drop what you are doing and respond. Your spouse complains about that thing he or she always complains about in that all-too-common complaining tone, and you respond in the same way you've always responded. Someone cuts you off in traffic, and you have your instinctual response.

Life comes at you, and you react. This is how all of us navigate life much of the time. And it mostly works for us. It helps us accomplish our goals, participate on teams, lead others, and maintain relationships. Much of what we do, we do "mindlessly"—we don't have to think about it. Did you have to think about how to get to work this morning? Did your workout require much brainpower? When your boss asked you for your monthly report, did you have to stop and think before you answered?

Probably not. We "know" how to do these things. As a result, we tend to get a lot of things done because we don't have to stop and concentrate on every task before us. Autopilot mechanisms on planes enable pilots to be more efficient. While still flying the plane, they can do other work. Or they can rest (figure 2).

Figure 2. Autopilot on: acting and reacting in the same way leads to the same results.

In the same way, "mindless" autopilot mode helps leaders get things done. Until it doesn't.

Autopilot—doing things the way you've always done them and reacting to people and situations the way you've always reacted—usually leads to getting the same results you've always gotten. Growth and change are about *new* results. You've probably heard that the definition of insanity is doing things the way you've always done them and expecting a different outcome. So to expect new results without addressing our autopilot responses is, in a word, crazy.

Autopilot and growth don't go together. Growth is about doing things differently in the hope of attaining a different outcome. If you, as a leader, want different results from yourself and from your people, you will have to act and react differently. You must disengage the autopilot and mindfully consider a different way of showing up and leading. New behaviors lead to new outcomes. It is "insane" to think you can grow otherwise (figure 3)!

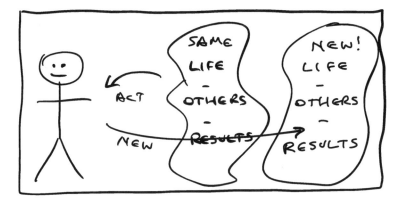

Figure 3. Autopilot off: acting and reacting in new ways leads to new results.

Roadblock 2: Leading with Less Than 100 Percent of Ourselves

Many leaders think that, in order to grow, they need to look outside themselves for instruction on how to lead better. So they go to a seminar. They pick up a book that other leaders recommend. They listen to a podcast on leadership. Or they hire a coach.

Why do they look outside themselves for answers? Because, on autopilot, they're accustomed to relying on only part of themselves. When they can't find the answer within themselves, they look to others.

Some of us rely only on our intellect, our ability to intimidate, or our emotional connection as we lead, thinking this single dimension is our whole self. What we don't realize is that if we could access 100 percent of ourselves—all four dimensions—we have a whole lot more of ourselves at our disposal to help us lead better.

Sometimes leaders who hire me as a coach think that I am going to teach them new ways to be a better leader. Instead, a lot of what I do as a coach is simply redirect their attention back on themselves, to become more self-aware. With their autopilot turned off, they can begin to see themselves in new ways. They begin to see they have more resources within themselves.

Growing as a leader is about more than learning how to "dress for success." Or raising your emotional quotient. Or getting smarter in a leadership subject area like delegation or time management or communication. Leadership growth encompasses all of those things and more!

But for you to lead like you were meant to, you must be more aware of who shows up when you show up. Leading with 100 percent of yourself means recognizing that when you walk into the room, four distinct aspects of yourself walk in with you and contribute to who you are as a leader.

> **For you to lead like you were meant to, you must be more aware of who shows up when you show up.**

Later, I will devote entire chapters to each of these four dimensions, but for now let me summarize: to be at your best—to lead with your best—you must be aware of how you show up in your *physical* body; your *intellectual* mind; your *emotional* heart; and, deep underneath these three, your *spiritual* essence—who you are and why you are here.

So it isn't just about relying on only one or two of your dimensions, like looking good (physical) or being smarter than everyone else (intellectual). To lead others well, you must lead yourself well. Leading yourself means being aware of and showing up at your best in all four dimensions—100 percent!

Roadblock 3: Failing to See How Our Greatest Strengths Connect to Our Greatest Weaknesses

Even for leaders who have turned off their autopilot and tuned in to 100 percent of all four dimensions, there is one final obstacle to growing and becoming their very best—failing to see the relationship between their greatest strengths and their greatest weaknesses.

In my coaching, I spend up to ninety days helping a leader discover how to get past this obstacle. Why does it take so long? First, we spend time overcoming roadblocks 1 and 2. Then it takes more time to sift through lots of surface symptoms before making our way down to core sources of the symptoms. Inevitably, the core sources contain two sides of the leader— their greatest strengths and their weaknesses that sabotage those great strengths.

In chapter 8, "My Default Dimension," I provide you with three examples of this yin and yang of greatest strength and greatest weakness. For now, let's use this example. Suppose you are a carpenter, and your great strength is hammering. Among your circle of friends, which includes other carpenters, you are the best with a hammer. You are the fastest. You are the most accurate. You can hammer the longest. You get hired and paid more because of your hammering talent. When anyone needs something hammered, they think of you first. Hammering is clearly your greatest strength.

One way your strength with a hammer becomes your weakness is when you insist on hammering all the time. Your boss would like you to saw some boards occasionally, but you insist on hammering only. Your wife wants to go out to din- ner, but you sit in the restaurant and hammer away. Your kids want you to play with them, but the only play you enjoy is with a hammer. Your friends, even your carpenter friends, stop spending time with you because they don't enjoy hammering all the time like you do.

This is a silly example, but it describes many leaders. In ways obvious, and in many ways more subtle, this is a glimpse of how your greatest strength and your greatest weakness are related to one another. Until you see this relationship for what it is, guess what? You will keep repeating the great weakness. Why? Because, of course, you want to repeat the great strength. Both are tied to the same trait in you. Seeing this roadblock and dealing with it will enable you to spend more time leveraging the strength and less time sabotaging yourself with the weakness.

GETTING PAST THE ROADBLOCKS

As I mentioned earlier, we will devote the most time to awareness. Why so much time? Because it is what is necessary to break through the three roadblocks to leadership growth!

I remember sitting down with a CEO not long after I had started coaching six of his executives. His first comment to me was "The word on Rob McKinnon is that he slows things down." At first, I wasn't sure if he was complimenting or criticizing me. But what he said was true. My first job as a coach is to help leaders turn off their autopilot. Autopilot is a useful shortcut for getting a lot of things done quickly. But autopilot blocks self-awareness. One of the biggest things I help leaders do is slow down and be more aware of themselves. This helps them lead mindfully instead of mindlessly.

When you become more aware of yourself, a whole new world of possibilities opens up. These new ways of showing up and behaving then lead to new outcomes. I have been surprised, and gratified, to see this happen in leaders time and time again—even in those leaders who already consider themselves very self-aware!

Once leaders gain greater self-awareness and see the new possibilities that go with it, much of my hard work as a coach is done! Why? Because these smart leaders quickly see easy changes they can make. A leader who sees that her anger is constantly triggered begins to understand how she alienates others. A leader who talks and talks recognizes he can do more listening. A leader who is hard on herself recognizes how she can be mercilessly hard on others.

> When you become more aware of yourself, a whole new world of possibilities opens up.

This new self-awareness inevitably reveals the low-hanging fruit of changes a leader can make immediately, as you'll discover in part 2.

So let's take the next step forward and learn more about being aware in four dimensions.

KEY TAKEAWAYS

- To lead better, I must contend with three roadblocks:

  - mindlessly thinking, feeling, seeing, saying, doing, and reacting the same ways I always have (being in autopilot)

  - failing to recognize and use 100 percent of myself

  - failing to see how my greatest weaknesses and my greatest strengths are wrapped around the same thing

- Autopilot is not necessarily bad. But when I'm on autopilot, doing things the way I've always done them, I will tend to get the same results. If I want to grow and see different results, I must turn off autopilot.

- If I want to grow, I need to lead more like who I am, rather than try to be someone else.

- Leading more like who I am begins with being more aware of four distinct parts of myself—my

physical body, my intellectual mind, my emotional heart, and my spiritual core.

- One way my great strength becomes a great weakness is when I insist on using the great strength
all the time, in every situation.

- The key to getting past the three roadblocks is to
slow down and become more aware.

- When I become more aware, a whole new world
of possibilities opens up for how I lead.

QUESTIONS FOR REFLECTION

- Think about the last time you failed to lead as well as you would have liked. What role did autopilot play?

- When have you been on autopilot today? What was the outcome?

- When is the last time you considered the role your body plays in your leadership presence? Your emotions? Your thoughts?

- To what degree are you aware that your greatest strength and greatest weakness share something in common?

- What grade would you give yourself for self-awareness today? Why?

CHAPTER 2

THE FOUR-DIMENSIONAL LEADER

Certain truths can be learned, it seems, only as one is sufficiently emptied, frightened, or confused.

—Belden C. Lane, *The Solace of Fierce Landscapes*

It is a sad fate for a man to die too well known to everybody else, and still unknown to himself.

—Francis Bacon

I was sitting in an airport lounge in New York, waiting to catch a flight home, when my friend Henry called. Henry is a serial entrepreneur. Our friendship dates back to grad school, and over the years we have done work together at the various companies he's been leading. After catching up briefly, he got to the point of his call.

"Rob, I've got this great chief operating officer. Last year he stripped twelve million dollars in operating expenses, made us more efficient, and today our results are better than ever. But I've heard complaints about how he treats his subordinates.

I've been told that he's a bully, that he intimidates. Some of his people have gone on record with HR that he creates a hostile work environment.

"I've talked with him about it. He's aware of this feedback and says he's working hard to be nice. But still, I keep getting these complaints. I'm starting to realize this is bigger than me. I can't coach him to get him where he needs to be. I was wondering if you could work with him. See if he can make some changes as a leader. I need the results he is able to get, but I also need him to treat his people better, or we are going to have some real problems."

And then Henry summed up his dilemma with this: "As smart as this guy is, he's having trouble figuring out how to get better."

LEADING STARTS WITH BEING

Any leader who can't first lead him- or herself is going to have trouble leading others. But what is the basic framework for leading yourself? Where do you start?

The US military is a good place to look. They are in the business of making leaders and helping those leaders get better. After all, the consequences under military leadership are more significant than most civilian leaders will ever face: peoples' lives are at stake.

Spend about seventeen dollars and pick up a copy of the Army's bible on leadership, FM 22-100: *The U.S. Army Leadership Field Manual*. In the opening chapter, you will find this succinct three-word summary of what the Army considers the most critical components of leadership: "BE. KNOW. DO."[3]

Notice that it begins with "be." Knowing and doing come next. Great leadership begins with who you are. Unless you get the "be" part right, the knowing and doing will be compromised.

No one else can "be" who you are as a leader. No one else can "become" who you might become as a leader. No one else can make you behave the way you behave, think your thoughts, feel your feelings, or possess your beliefs and convictions.

But what do you do with this notion of "being" a leader? It sounds so passive. So irrelevant. So boring. But it is the absolute beginning point for highly effective leaders. Get the "being" right, and all your knowing and doing will have a much greater impact. By the end of this book, you will realize there is so much more to you as a leader, and you have so much more capacity to lead than you are using right now.

> **Great leadership begins with who you are.**

To demonstrate that you have a greater capacity to lead than you realize, I would like you to stop reading briefly to do this exercise. If you stop and do it, you will be glad you did. If you skip it now and keep reading, it will not be as powerful or helpful to you later.

MY RECENT REGRETTABLE LEADERSHIP EXPERIENCE

Think back over the past couple of weeks to an encounter that did not go well, in which you regret how you handled yourself. This encounter could be any interaction with another person or group of people—your boss, a colleague, or a direct report. It could be a meeting that you led or participated in. It could be a talk or presentation that you gave. The key is that it did not go well. You wish you could have a do-over.

Write down everything you can remember about how you showed up in that encounter.

I will invite you to return to this exercise in each of the next four chapters.

✑ "JOURNAL TIME"

Take five to eight minutes to write down everything you can remember about how you were showing up at your Recent Regrettable Leadership Experience that you wish you could do over.

WHAT IS A FOUR-DIMENSIONAL LEADER?

Leaders routinely bring some of their most challenging problems to their conversations with me. And I remind them: when something gets too difficult to figure out, break it into smaller parts.

That's where the four-dimensional leadership model helps us. Instead of getting overwhelmed by this big, amorphous, ill-defined notion of "being a better leader," we break "being a better leader" down into four smaller parts—physical, intellectual, emotional, and spiritual—which together capture the whole person of the leader. Figure 4 is a simple diagram to illustrate the four dimensions and their relationship to one another.

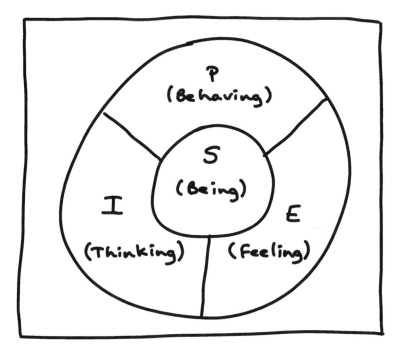

Figure 4. Diagram of the four-dimensional leader model.

We'll discuss this diagram in greater detail later. But for now, notice the outer three dimensions, which express your personality—how you think, feel, and behave. This is also where all your "doing" shows up.

Inside the intellectual, emotional, and physical dimensions, at the very center, is the spiritual. Just like the Army's leadership model, the four-dimensional leadership model, at its core, has to do with *being*.

The process of fully becoming a four-dimensional leader is gradual. There will be things for you to do. But the sooner you focus on being, the faster you will be a better leader. And as you become a four-dimensional leader, you will gain greater capacity to lead. With this greater capacity, you will begin "doing" more of the right things. And you will lead more like you were meant to lead.

A Four-Dimensional Leader in Action

I'd like you to watch an example of a leader who embodies the four dimensions of leadership in a very powerful way. Get a copy of the movie *Gladiator*,[4] and watch the first seven minutes. You're going to see General Maximus Decimus Meridius, a great portrait of a leader played by Russell Crowe, preparing for a tough day at the office. His leadership effectiveness, based on who he "is," will greatly impact the lives of his men. Though Maximus is a fictional character, he offers an ideal four-dimensional visual of a great leader.

Watch the clip with a pen and paper in hand, and notice how he leads himself at the very beginning, mostly while he is still by himself, isolated from his soldiers. Write down everything you notice about how he fortifies himself—leads himself and then his soldiers—before the battle even begins.

So lay this book down, watch the clip, and make notes.

📝 **"JOURNAL TIME"**

When you can, take about eight minutes to find and watch the opening scenes of Gladiator. *Record all you notice about how Russell Crowe's character, Maximus, prepares to lead in his difficult day ahead.*

What did you notice?

Here's what I observed after watching this clip a few times. With each observation, using parentheses, I noted the dimensions I saw in Maximus: physical (P), intellectual (I), emotional (E), and spiritual (S).

The opening frames reveal only the hand of a man as he walks through a sunny field of wheat ready for harvest. He gently brushes the heads of wheat. As he continues, we begin to hear the laughter of little children in the background.

Then the camera cuts to a close-up of General Maximus's face, slowly turning upward as his eyes open. We realize the previous image in the field represents a vision of a place he traveled to in his mind, likely his own fields with the playful sounds of his own son nearby. But we quickly see he is now standing in the ruin and carnage of a war zone, with fires still smoldering from the previous day's battles.

What is he doing in this opening scene to prepare to lead his men? I suggest he is meditating on his identity (S) as a farmer first and a warrior second, and that this reflection helps him prepare for a final speech he will give to his soldiers just before the battle commences. As much as he is willing to give his life on this day to lead his soldiers to success, he still longs to be in his peaceful fields, harvesting his wheat. He also connects with his primary role in life as father to his son and the safe and sunny place he is in, far from the grim battlefield. We see a face that appears tired and muddy (P) but at peace and resolved (E). The scene suggests his serious contemplation (I) on the leadership tasks he has ahead of him in the coming hours.

He turns to leave his place of meditation. But before he goes, he glimpses a small bird perched on a branch near the ground, with smoke drifting by in the background. He studies the bird and watches as it flits away, unbound by the war zone. The corner of his mouth rises in a slight grin. The slight grin suggests a moment of levity (E), as he sees something that is fully alive and free amid the death and darkness of the battlefield.

Maximus ends his quiet reflection and strides (P) toward his troops, who are making final preparations for battle. He is clearly a warrior, a soldier's soldier, clad in armor with animal skins layered over his broad shoulders for warmth (P). Dirt and grime (P) suggest he has been in the thick of it with his men.

As he passes them, he looks each in the eye. One by one, they greet him with a single salutation: "General!" He pauses with one and gently bumps the soldier's chest with his fist (P).

Before we have heard him say anything, we behold a leader (S)—confident, peaceful, and strong.

Walking up to his second-in-command, Quintus, he speaks for the first time, assessing the condition of his men: "Lean and hungry."

Quintus shouts to correct someone. "Soldier, I ordered you to move those catapults forward. They are out of range."

"The range is good," (I) Maximus advises in a low voice (P).

"But the danger to the cavalry . . . ," Quintus argues.

"Is good. Agreed?" responds Maximus. As the battle later unfolds, we will see that it is Maximus who leads the cavalry and puts himself and them at risk in the line of the catapults' fire.

In this simple exchange, Maximus displays multiple dimensions. First, he knows exactly the range of the catapults and where they need to be placed to be highly effective in combination with the cavalry charge that will surprise the enemy (I). Second, he is courageous (E) in facing the risk of "friendly fire," and he has calculated that the risk is worth the opportunity. Also, he does not override Quintus with anger (E) but simply makes the correction quietly so as to not undermine or embarrass Quintus in front of the soldiers.

Quintus and Maximus stand awaiting the Germans' response to an offer of surrender. The Germans instead send the messenger back on his horse, beheaded. They shout curses and mock Maximus's soldiers, goading them to a fight.

Quintus, with contempt, says, "People should know when they are conquered."

But Maximus responds, "Would you [know], Quintus? Would I?" He seems to speak with humility, deep understanding, and sympathy for the human condition (S).

Then Maximus bends down, scoops up some dirt from the ground, rubs it in his hands, and sniffs it. Multiple interpretations could be drawn here. But I believe he is once again reconnecting with his core identity as a farmer (S), which he will mention in his speech in the very next scene. He is here as a warrior for today; he and his men will kill and be killed, but when it is done, he will return to his fields and his love of farming.

As he leaves Quintus to join his cavalry troops, Maximus departs with the words "strength and honor," which resound as the soldiers' motto as they repeat the words to one another. Strength and honor speak of character (S).

General Maximus gallops by horseback through the line of troops. Moved by his leadership presence (P, I, E, and S!), the soldiers rise to their feet. They seem ready to follow him wherever he leads.

Finally, just before kicking off the battle, Maximus gathers with his cavalrymen in a grove of trees away from the front lines and proceeds to give a profoundly motivational speech preparing them for what they are about to face:

"Fratres [brothers]!" The soldiers respond with cheers. "Three weeks from now, I will be harvesting my crops. Imagine where you will be, and it will be so. Hold the line! Stay with me! If you find yourself alone, riding in green fields with the sun on your face, do not be troubled. For you are in Elysium[5] [laughter], and you're already dead! Brothers . . . what we do in life . . . echoes in eternity!"

Maximus has been preparing all morning to give his speech to this group of soldiers who will deliver the risky but surprise knockout punch of the battle. And we see he does it in a fully four-dimensional way. He sits atop his horse as a physical role model of the courageous leader who inspires his men to follow him into the arrows and spears of the enemy. He addresses the emotional gravity of the challenge with levity and tells them to not be afraid. These soldiers already know the technical details of their job, but he gives the final critical instructions (I) of "Hold the line! Stay with me!" And as he finishes, he connects with them soul to soul (S) with a reminder of the significance of their actions, their bravery in battle—that success or failure today will impact others tomorrow. What a powerful display of leadership—and he speaks only sixty-four words! The power of his four-dimensional presence says so much more.

When was the last time you had a significant speech to deliver to your troops? What was at stake? How many words did you have to use? How much were you able to inspire or persuade merely by your presence?

As you learn to expand your capacity to lead, to draw fully on all that is available to you as a leader, you are going to realize there is far more available to you than you have been using. You are also going to discover the hidden aspects of yourself that have been sabotaging your strengths.

Who Walks Into the Room?

We've been observing Russell Crowe in the role of General Maximus. Now, let's turn our attention to you.

Who walks into the room when you, as a leader, walk into the room? You might hear this as a rhetorical question. But until you master the ability to observe yourself, your presence, as others do, you don't have a full perspective on how you impact others as their leader.

If you say, "It's just me—I walk into the room," then your perspective is very one-dimensional. And you don't realize that you are affecting others in the room with more than just that one dimension. By not understanding how you are affecting others in ways you cannot see, you forego the opportunity to be at your best, perform at your best, and get the best results.

Here's what I see when you walk into the room. (By the way, your followers see most of this as well.)

Physical. When you enter the room, before you even open your mouth, you have changed the room. The energy has changed, just as it does when one person walks up to a small group of people chatting at a reception. You have either added to it or taken away from it with your physical presence. You may have a large presence in the room, or you may have a small presence.

Depending on how you walk in, whether striding, shuffling, or something in between, people may make room for you automatically, or they may not even notice you. Certainly, I'll be able to discern something about you based on what you're wearing and how you're wearing it.

You tell me a lot just by your physical presence: how you're standing, for instance—feet together or apart, stomach relaxed or tight, shoulders hunched forward or pulled backward, and whether your head leans forward or tilts to one side. And certainly, your face reveals something about what mood you're in and whether you're thinking hard about something.

You tell me a lot just by your physical presence in the room.

Intellectual. Then you open your mouth. Once you do this and words start to come out, I begin to get a sense of *what* you are thinking about. I can detect your most prominent thoughts. They are probably things you want me to think about as well, since you are expressing them to me. Simultaneously, I get clues about *why* they are your dominant thoughts in this moment.

As I continue to listen, I get a sense of *how* you process thoughts, whether they are systematic and logical, or random and creative. I will begin to take my measure of your intellectual presence, whether you are incredibly bright, an intellectual blowhard, or somewhere in between.

Emotional. As I study your posture and the expression on your face and listen to the tone and volume of your voice, I also begin to get clues about your emotional state. I sense whether you are happy and lighthearted, at peace with yourself and your circumstances, or sad, angry, frustrated, or fearful in the moment.

I remember that emotions can be a little deceptive. You could be smiling on the outside while you're in great pain on the inside. You may be very good at fooling people in this area. But generally, I'll look to see if the emotion I detect lines up with the words I'm hearing and what you are doing with your body when you say them. I'm looking for consistency and authenticity.

Over time, I can tell a lot about how you're feeling just by carefully listening and watching.

Spiritual. This is the one area where you could really fool me. I can sense the other three dimensions with my own eyes and ears, but I may or may not gain clarity on this hidden dimension without spending a lot of time with you.

I'm not looking for what religion you're practicing—though you may reveal that. More significantly, I'm looking to discern what your core beliefs, your values, and the foundation of your character are. In the spiritual dimension, I'm trying to discern the essence of who you are—your purpose and calling in life.

It can be especially hard for me to detect this when times are good. It's when significant challenges come along that I stand the best chance of discerning your spiritual dimension. Clues for me are when I hear you say, "I believe . . ." or "We must do this. . . ."

Of course, it's also entirely possible that your spiritual presence is a vacuum and you cover it with the facade of the other three dimensions. But to achieve great and lasting results, your followers will demand authentic, four-dimensional leadership.

This is what I see when you walk into the room: you, in four dimensions. If all four dimensions line up cohesively, I will see you as authentic and probably be inclined to follow you. But if one dimension doesn't match the others, I will be skeptical and hesitant to follow you. If you say all the right things (intellectually) but don't express them with passion (emotionally), I might question whether you really have any conviction (spiritually) about what you are saying, and thus I will question whether I should follow you.

On the other hand, if you emote intense enthusiasm but your ideas sound silly, I will think you are a clown and probably not follow you either. If you say smart things with enthusiasm and a smile on your face, yet I know you have lied in the past, I will doubt whether things will really be different this time.

> To achieve great and lasting results, your followers will demand authentic, four-dimensional leadership.

I'm watching you, listening to you, and sensing you. And regardless of whether either of us is aware that I am doing it in four dimensions, my decision to follow you as a leader enthusiastically will hinge on whether all four line up.

Can you fool me for a while? Certainly the first time, and maybe the second. But eventually, I will catch on to you. And while I may have to suffer with you as my leader, and do my work dutifully in order to keep my job and collect a paycheck, you will not inspire my best performance, and I will be looking for another leader to follow—probably in another organization.

In fact, it's likely I am more finely attuned to your presence than you are. Your big disadvantage? You are on autopilot, and you are not fully aware of what all four of your dimensions are saying to me.

In the next four chapters, we will look at each of your four dimensions in detail, beginning with the physical. Turn off autopilot by digging in, paying attention, and noticing how much more effectively you can lead when you lead yourself.

KEY TAKEAWAYS

- To get better as a leader, I should focus more on being "who I actually am," not just knowing and doing.

- How I get better as a leader can feel like solving a big problem. The easiest way to solve a big problem is to break it down into smaller parts.

- I have four dimensions as a leader—physical, intellectual, emotional, and spiritual, with the spiritual at the core of my being.

- When I walk into the room, all four dimensions add up to represent me as a leader. My challenge is to be aware of all four and show up well.

❓ QUESTIONS FOR REFLECTION

- Practice drawing and labeling our basic diagram (figure 4) to illustrate the four dimensions. (Remember P, I, E, and S.)

- Reflect on the last time you had a significant talk, presentation, or conversation. What did you do to prepare for it? How much of this preparation was about knowing? How much was about doing? How much was simply about your presence (being)?

- What have your four dimensions communicated about you as you have interacted with others in the past twenty-four hours?

- **Go to LeadLikeYouBook.com for additional exercises related to this chapter.**

CHAPTER 3

THE PHYSICAL DIMENSION

Mr. Duffy lived a short distance from his body.
—James Joyce

Pain plus reflection equals progress.
—Ray Dalio

John grimaced. His eyes narrowed to slits. His eyebrows pointed down toward his nose. His jaw clenched. Everyone around him felt guilty in his presence, as if they had done something wrong.

Laura talked. And talked. And talked some more. She dominated conversations by never giving up the airwaves. Her staff reported they didn't feel heard and didn't feel their opinions mattered. Many ignored her as she droned on.

Allen erupted. He would be sitting quietly and all of a sudden use his face, his body, and his voice as if they were weapons—shouting, waving his fists, and intimidating others by moving into their personal space. His coworkers spoke of "walking on eggshells" in his presence. Meetings he led were quiet. No one wanted to be his target of the day.

I worked with each of these leaders—leaders whose physical presence and behavior were sabotaging their leadership effectiveness. Either they invited me in because they weren't getting the results they wanted or their board or boss asked me to work with them. They were simply behaving the way they always had. But now their behavior was no longer working for them the way it had in the past.

As you think about being at your best as a leader, begin with the dimension that is the most obvious and yet the most easily ignored—your body. Ignoring your body is a sure sign you're on autopilot. So turn off your autopilot, and tune in to your physical self. Your capacity to lead, to influence others, starts in your body.

How? First, notice the ways you take in data through your body. Your body tunes in to the people and activities around you so you can determine what kind of leadership the moment demands of you.

Second, notice how you send out data through your body. Your body makes everything happen:

- Your mouth speaks.
- Your feet walk you into the room.
- Your eyes look around.
- Your hands gesture and type.
- Your face tightens or relaxes.

Your leadership won't go anywhere, won't be expressed, and won't reach others without your body. No one will know your great passions, your wise thoughts, or what you care deeply about without the expression of your body. And how can your true identity be revealed without an animated body?

You express everything through your body. If your body breaks down, your ability to express yourself breaks down, which means you cannot lead at your best.

Think about a significant leadership event coming up for you in the next few weeks. This could be a major presentation, a meeting with a big client or prospect, or a strategy retreat that you lead—anything where you are going to be front and center in your role as a leader. Picture yourself in this future setting, and think about how you want to show up physically. What do you want your body to project? How do you want to connect with others? What impression do you want to make? All of this will be done through your body, so you must be self-aware physically.

Three aspects of physical awareness are critical for you as a leader:

- understanding how your physical presence speaks to others
- knowing that being at your leadership best begins with being at your physical best
- learning to "listen" when your body "speaks" to you in ways your mind and heart cannot

Leaders on autopilot can be oblivious to all three with potentially disastrous results.

Let's look at how to be better in all three of these aspects of your physical dimension.

PHYSICAL PRESENCE: HOW YOUR BODY SPEAKS

All of us, at some level, are tuned in to our appearance. It's why we put clothes on before we walk out the door.

But your awareness of your presence could be superficial. For instance, you might consider yourself a sharp dresser. Your shirts and shoes are in style, bought from the right stores with the right labels. You know the current "correct" length for your skirts or pants, or whether pleats or cuffs are in or out. You have your power suits. You have your casual wear. All are intended to make you look good for the audience of the day.

In the end, clothes, shoes, and hairstyles are all window dressing. They have their place. But many leaders are way too tuned in to what they're wearing and out of touch with the body doing the wearing.

Your presence speaks to those you lead. Presence is about how you show up—in your body.

One way to become more aware of your presence is to ask yourself, "What does my body say when I am not speaking?" Presence does include your voice, but many times we think we use only our voice to speak to others. In reality, voice is just one part of your physical presence.

What does my body say when I am not speaking?

Have you ever been on an airplane where you see a movie but you can't hear the sound? You watch for a little bit to see if you can figure out what is going on.

Think about all you are able to discern by observing the actors' bodies without being able to hear their voices. You can tell if they are happy or sad, playing or working, stressed or relaxed, and directing others or following. After watching for a while, you may be able to tell who the good guys are and who the bad guys are. All of this without hearing their voices—just from observing their physical presence.

Do you have a meeting with two or more people today? If so, test your observational skills live and in person. For a few moments, try hitting the "mute" button in your mind, and stop listening to what they are saying with their voices. Instead, tune in to what they are saying with their bodies.

Are they leaning toward or away from one another? Are they highly expressive or expressionless in their faces? Are they engaged or detached? Observe as much as you can, and notice your interpretations of what they must be thinking or feeling at the moment. Notice whether you are drawn toward them or prefer to keep your distance.

This exercise of observing others, whether in movies or in person, is merely a warm-up for observing your own physical presence. I know many leaders who are really good at tuning in to others but very poor at tuning in to themselves. To get better as a leader, you need to be more aware of your physical self.

So try this. Stand or sit in front of a mirror and do a top-to-bottom body scan. Really notice yourself—perhaps for the first time in a long time. See yourself the way others see you every day.

Start at the top. What's going on with your face? Is your forehead relaxed? Or is it scrunched up, like you're studying or thinking really hard? What about your eyes? Is your gaze soft and welcoming, or penetrating? Are your eyes fully open, or narrowed into slits? Which way are they looking? Can they stay fixed on an object—in this case, you? Or do they blink and look away? Is your jaw tight, or relaxed? How about your mouth? Again, do you see tight, pursed lips? Or are they relaxed?

Overall, what does your face convey? That you're interested, peaceful, or happy? Or aloof, judgmental, intense, or arrogant? What would this face telegraph to you if you were seeing it for the first time? This is the face that all of your followers are studying and reading every day. What messages does it convey?

Continue the scan downward. How is your head positioned on your neck, over your torso? Is it leaning forward? Backward? To one side? Or balanced and centered?

How about your shoulders? Are they tensed upward, tight, and into the body? Pushed back? Hunched forward? Or relaxed? What about your chest? Is it sticking out, or caved in?

Your shoulders probably dictate where your arms are hanging. Are they hanging toward your back? Toward your stomach? Or are they spread out from your side, like you're about to grab a pair of six-shooters out of your holsters?

What about your stomach? Are you sucking it in? Or relaxing, letting it all hang out? Overall, how is your torso positioned over your waist and hips? Does it tilt to one side? Does it lean forward? Or away?

Finally, how are you standing? Ramrod straight, as if at attention? Or slouching? Or somewhere in between? Are your feet together, or apart? Which way are they pointing?

What do you make of this person before you? You might as well ask the question of yourself, because everyone in your organization is doing it as they see you.

As you notice some features you hadn't noticed before, be curious and ask yourself, "What makes me stand that way? What causes me to have that look on my face? Does the way I look on the outside reflect what I'm thinking or feeling on the inside?"

I regularly use this method to introduce leaders to themselves. Invariably, they notice something for the first time.

Just last week, I had a session with Tom, a CEO with whom I have only been working a couple of months. To help him grow in self-awareness, I asked him my typical question: "Tell me about an incident from the past week where you were either at your best or at your worst." I encourage leaders to evaluate themselves at the extremes because I find this is more conducive to learning self-awareness.

Tom immediately had a story for me. He had been monitoring an email exchange between two of his senior executives regarding the implementation of a new initiative at the company. As he read each successive email, he realized that one executive, his COO, "got it" and was on the right track, while the second executive, his CFO, was simply creating delays and roadblocks. Finally, Tom said, he read a response from the CFO that "broke the camel's back"—an interesting choice of words.

I then asked him, "What do you recall happening in your body, physically, at that point?"

He thought and then replied, "Well, I gritted my teeth." As he said this, he replicated it in front of me—clenching his jaw, tilting his head downward, and narrowing his eyes. "And then I got up out of my chair and walked down to his office." Tom is a big guy, probably six foot two and 250-plus pounds. He can have an imposing physical presence without trying very hard.

"And what was that about?" I asked.

"Well, I just felt that a simple reply by email at this point wouldn't do it. I needed to confront him face to face."

Do you see how much of Tom's response came from his physical dimension? Even sitting alone at his desk with no one present, his muscles tightened as if he was getting ready to fight. And he carried that presence out of his office and into the office of the subordinate he wanted to confront.

So begin to notice yourself in a new way, and consider how you want to present yourself to those you lead. Turn off the autopilot in the morning by tuning in to your physical presence, and when you're done checking your hair, linger for an additional minute or two and consider what "game face" you want to put on for the day.

How about the rest of your body? I suggest you start by simply filling out all three of your physical dimensions— your height, width, and depth. Fully stand, comfortably and balanced, in your body. This is the beginning stance. Make adjustments from here—intentional adjustments, not autopilot adjustments.

Throughout the day, notice what your body is doing in relation to others. Do you face someone squarely, giving him or her 100 percent of yourself—your full attention? Or does just your torso face the person while your legs and feet point in another direction, letting him or her know you're itching to move on? When you're having lunch with someone or at a reception, is your body present and still while your eyes are roaming elsewhere?

People, when they see you, are sizing you up as a leader. And they have two questions in their subconscious. Within the first seconds they meet you, before you even open your mouth, they are forming a first impression. That first impression answers their first question: "Do I like you?"

As minutes pass, they look and listen to see whether "the audio matches the video." Do your words align with your actions? This assessment answers their second question: "Do I trust you?" Leading others begins with leading yourself. Leading yourself requires self-awareness and seeing yourself as others see you.

PHYSICAL BEST: READY TO LEAD

A few seconds into the call, I knew the leader on the other end was in trouble.

"Rob, I'm not in very good shape for this call," Roberta said. "I've been sick but 'powering through' the past four days. I can't slow down—too many deadlines. They are expecting me to be there."

She sounded like a mess. Her words came slowly. There were long pauses between sentences. At times, she just wasn't making sense. She continued downloading a long list of negatives.

"And the worst part is . . . I just learned they want to move my team's office to another part of the building! I was just getting settled into the office space where we moved six months ago. They can't do this! It is such a stupid decision! I can't believe they are trying to do this to us! I'm going to fight it!"

She didn't sound like she was in any condition to fight anybody. The more we talked, the more I realized this leader, who on her better days was on a fast track to the C-suite, was at this moment totally broken down physically. Her body was giving up. She had been sick but had kept going the past few days. Now she could go no further. And what else was happening? Her emotions were in a downward spiral, and she could hardly think straight. Her chief obsession was fighting a proposed office space change, when I knew she had bigger issues on her plate.

I spoke to her more forcefully than I usually do as a coach. "Have your assistant clear your calendar. Go home and go to bed." Until she gave her body a break, and let it heal, she would have no chance to think clearly and lead well.

Your body is the vehicle that delivers your leadership. If your body is broken down, you will not lead at your best, if at all. You need to take care of your body, and you need to listen to it. It has a lot to tell you, including, as we will see, how to lead better.

I remember a friend of mine who drove a high-end SUV that was only two years old. I listened with amazement as he told me about having to replace the engine. It had developed an oil leak that at first went undetected and then (even after the "check engine" light came on and stayed on) was ignored. He ignored it all the way to the side of the road one day when the vehicle literally ground to a halt and couldn't take him any farther.

How does this happen? Besides the dashboard indicators, I would imagine the engine must have acted sluggish and would have begun to make some different sounds toward the end—warning signs to the driver to pay attention, look under the hood, and go see a mechanic. But instead, my friend just stepped on the gas and kept going—until he couldn't.

This is how many leaders treat their bodies, especially the leaders who are "successful." They boast of their busyness. They run on too little sleep and too much adrenaline. They drink too much alcohol, considering it a reward for working hard. They continue to work long after they have left the office, including on vacations. They ignore all the little pain signals until their doctor has a serious talk with them. Even then, many continue to think they are immortal, that they will only be running this hard for another year or two, and then they will rest. Then they will get back in balance.

You don't show up at your best every day when you lead this way. You can wash your face and put on a fresh shirt in the morning, but the vehicle underneath is still suffering and wearing down—not at its best.

You probably got suckered into this pattern. You learned you could survive all-nighters in college, so you took it into your job. You read stories of CEOs of big global companies jetting all over the place, and you figure you should do the same. Your mantra is that you should be the first in and the last out, setting the example for others. Money is made through hard work, so shouldn't you, as leader, be working the hardest? After a while, it becomes a part of your image, working yourself to exhaustion. Proving yourself to . . . somebody. Over time, you get lulled into believing this is normal. It has become a habit—a bad habit.

But it's not sustainable. And you are not leading with your best. If you pause, turn off the autopilot, and take a hard look at yourself, you will see it. Maybe. A lot of leaders have to experience a breakdown of some kind—where they hit the barrier and finally realize it's impacting their performance.

The breakdown may be physical (sluggishness, lack of energy), emotional (feelings of being down or discouraged), or intellectual (fogginess, jumbled thinking). But more often than not, its roots can be traced back to you physically abusing your body.

Think about the last time you had an uncontrolled emotional outburst or made a very bad decision. Odds are you were in rough shape physically at the time—extremely tired, stressed, hungry, or intoxicated. It is interesting to me that addiction recovery programs use the acronym HALT as a reminder for the conditions in which we are most vulnerable— when we are hungry, angry, lonely, or tired. Two of these four vulnerabilities—hungry and tired—are squarely in the physical dimension.

> Manage your energy so you peak for the sprints. Rest and replenish in between.

I love the paradigm that Jim Loehr and Tony Schwartz use in their excellent book, *The Power of Full Engagement*, which is also about the four dimensions. They liken you, the leader, to an athlete. And your leadership challenge is to manage your energy. Don't view your day or week as a marathon—using a consistent amount of energy over a long stretch of time. Instead, view the day ahead as a series of sprints. Manage your energy so you peak for the sprints. Rest and replenish in between.

How fit to lead are you? This is a question that has long-term, as well as day-to-day, implications.

A few years ago, I was coaching a CEO, Allen, who had a major sales presentation coming up. He asked me to help him get ready for it. Given the size of the potential sale, he wanted to be at his very best.

You might think we would start with the persuasive talking points in his sales presentation or the layout of his PowerPoint deck. No. Instead, I asked him about his travel plans.

Allen lived in Washington, DC. His presentation was in downtown Chicago, midmorning. Allen's plan was to catch the first flight of the day from DC, take advantage of the one-hour time change, and arrive at O'Hare in time to travel downtown and still have an hour to spare before his meeting.

What kind of physical shape do you think he would be in for one of his biggest presentations of the year? Think about it. Having to wake up around 4:00 a.m. to make it to the airport on time, he would not get a full night's rest. He would probably compensate for this with a restless nap on the flight or extra caffeine to stay awake. Breakfast would likely be junk. And the only exercise that morning would be the hustle through the airport. Bottom line, he's walking into the meeting with significantly less than his very best—when it really counts.

So we strategized. He decided to treat the meeting like game day and pay as much attention to his physical preparation as an NFL player getting ready for Sunday. Turning off the autopilot and reflecting a little, he realized he could take a flight the evening before the meeting and stay overnight, thus ensuring he had plenty of rest and preparation.

When we debriefed it the next week, Allen told me that he had arrived in Chicago and slept well the night before, woke up and worked out, and had a healthy breakfast in the hotel, which was a few blocks from where the big meeting was going to take place. When he walked into the meeting with his team, he felt he was really on his game. The presentation that followed was successful, and they had a handshake deal before leaving the room.

When you think about attributes that were critical to Allen performing at a high level in that meeting—focus, confidence, clarity, and strength—you recognize he had a much better chance of possessing these by being at his physical best.

PHYSICAL WISDOM: WHAT YOUR BODY IS TELLING YOU

Besides presence and fitness, leaders should recognize their bodies' signals and know how to react to them. Later, we will look at how leaders use the mental intelligence of their minds and the emotional intelligence of their hearts to discern how to lead. But leaders may not recognize the physical intelligence their bodies offer in the form of gut instinct.

Can you recall a time when you, or someone with you, were suddenly confronted with danger, like stepping in front of a moving car? You weren't injured, but in the split second before, you sensed you were going to be. Can you remember how your body reacted? How you were breathing? Your heart rate? I imagine both were rapid. How did you move? Did you run? Did you dodge? Did you pull back? Did you even have to think about what to do? Or did your body move you out of harm's way on its own?

All of these are examples of your body acting on its own intelligence. In a split second, before you can think logically or even feel fear, your body has already processed the threat and equipped you with a burst of adrenaline to deal with what comes next. This same instinct that helped our ancient ancestors survive the saber-toothed tiger in more primitive times is still available to help you lead today. Are you aware of it? If not, that may be a signal you need to practice greater awareness in this area.

Our bodies can be speedy receptors of the most subtle signals. Leaders can learn to pay more attention to their bodies as sources of information. Our bodies will often let us know that someone or something should be feared—or embraced, or avoided, or protected, or started, or stopped—*before* logic or emotion sends us the same message.

Rachel, a CFO, told me about attending a board meeting to present financial results. It did not go well. One board member kept drilling her on several numbers in the income statement, not happy with the response she was providing. Neither the CEO nor anyone else in the room stepped in to assist her. It was just her and this one board member, going back and forth. She felt alone and vulnerable.

When I asked her what she was feeling in the midst of all that, instead of giving me an emotion like fear or anger, she said, "At first, I felt like fighting, but when the CEO didn't chime in to back me up, I felt like running away." Her "feeling" was a physical reaction—her body was saying to her, "Let's get out of here!"

Unfortunately, Rachel didn't pay attention to the message her gut, or body, was trying to send. If she had, she might have taken charge and said to her body, "Now hold on a moment. Take a few breaths. What kind of message will that send to everyone in the room if I just run away?"

Instead, as soon as the meeting was adjourned, Rachel gathered her notebooks and rushed out of the room without engaging further with any of the board members. Within minutes of leaving, she felt foolish and realized her behavior looked weak and reactive. As we debriefed her scenario, she realized the clues were there all along: her body was telling her what it wanted to do. If she had been more aware, she could have overruled her gut instinct and remained in the room.

Think about the last meeting you attended where one or more controversial topics were discussed. As everyone at the table weighed in with their thoughts, did you feel like leaning toward them or away? When they spoke, did you stay relaxed, or did you sense agitation somewhere? How did your body react to the topic being discussed? Did your gut instinct tell you anything in that moment?

Your body indicates its own involuntary processing of signals in a number of ways:

- breath
- heart rate
- muscle tension
- posture, position, and movement

All of these were originally wired into our bodies to help us survive in a world that was physically dangerous—filled with, among other things, carnivorous animals, harsh weather, or rival tribes. Today, danger and challenge still surround us; they're just a little more sophisticated—dissatisfied customers, selfish coworkers, and demanding bosses.

What is your gut instinct trying to tell you?

Practice tuning in more to your body and being aware of the signals it wants to send you. This physical awareness, taken together with your thoughts and feelings, will give you a strong and balanced platform from which to assess and adjust, as you'll learn to do in part 2.

In the meantime, here are two physical self-leadership challenges to help you manage all three aspects of your physical dimension, shift out of autopilot, and lead more effectively.

PHYSICAL SELF-LEADERSHIP CHALLENGE I: GET READY TO LEAD PHYSICALLY

✍ "JOURNAL TIME"

Go to LeadLikeYouBook.com for an exercise related to this challenge.

Physical fitness is a nearly $100 billion industry.[6] You have a wealth of resources readily available to help you be at your physical best to lead. Below are some of the key areas I find that consistently challenge leaders as they try to get better. When you consider that the physical dimension is one of the easiest of your dimensions to manage and improve, this self-leadership challenge is one you have to meet and overcome!

Get Enough Sleep

I doubt you get enough sleep as a leader. You prop yourself up with caffeine and run on adrenaline. Maybe you feed your ego by telling others you only get four to five hours of sleep per night. You're so busy! You have so much to do! Anyone with your level of responsibility would rise at five and go to sleep after midnight.

Well, that thinking may make you feel good about yourself, but your body disagrees. It wants to tell you to make sure you are recharging the batteries every night so you bring a fresh perspective and thinking to the challenges you face each day. Your stewardship demands that you have a clear head and an energized body to lead at your best. And sleep is not just for your body, the physical part of you. It's for your intellectual, emotional, and spiritual dimensions as well. They all need a periodic break.

Eat Right

Food impacts your performance, appearance, and energy level as a leader. If you want to perform at a high level, you would do well to think of your food intake as a corporate athlete would. Your daily performance as a leader is a series of matches. Some of them are team events; some are individual. And just as top athletes closely monitor their food and liquid intake before and during a contest, so should you.

Top athletes know just the right portions of the foods that suit them, and they have a good idea of when they will need to consume them relative to the start of the contest. Each athlete's diet is unique and based on experimenting over time to figure out what the body needs and how it will respond.

How much food is in your stomach right now? Too much? Not enough? Do you feel sluggish, or nimble? Bloated and heavy, or balanced and ready?

> **Need to lose weight? Burn more calories than you consume.**

Maryann Karinch, a former extreme athlete, wrote in her book *Diets Designed for Athletes* that "the world's best athletes don't eat the same way or use the same products—even those in the same sport—because they have learned over time what works precisely right for them."[7] You have got to figure out what foods work best for you.

How about your weight? According to the Centers for Disease Control and Prevention, 71 percent of adults are overweight.[8] The diet industry collects north of $50 billion a year from people looking for a quick-fix, can't-fail weight-loss plan.

I will charge you whatever you paid for this book to give you the bottom line in six words: burn more calories than you consume.

Of course, there are many ways to follow this guideline—types and quantities of foods, how they are prepared, when and how often you eat, and types and frequency of exercise. But at the end of the day, if you want to lose weight, this is the mathematical formula your body requires you to follow.

To simplify further, build some routine breakfasts, lunches, and snacks into your diet—foods you enjoy but that don't break the caloric bank. Carry healthy snacks like almonds or Cheerios with you when you travel so you avoid reaching for a candy bar or chips on an empty stomach.

Drink Right

Pay attention to what you're pouring into your body. Again, all things in moderation. You may depend on caffeine—whether in coffee, tea, or soft drinks—to wake up, get going, and stay alert. But when you begin drinking more and more caffeine stimulants later in the day, every day, you are propping yourself up and ignoring your body's drowsy signals that it needs more sleep. Wean yourself off this addiction, and get more sleep.

As you cut back on caffeine, drink more water or healthy, clear liquids. The common recommendation is "eight by eight"—or sixty-four ounces of water a day. There is no science to this number. A more observable measure for getting enough water is to drink until your urine is clear. Water helps cleanse your body from the inside. Plus, it reduces hunger pangs, diminishes bad breath, and keeps your mouth from going dry during all that public speaking you do.

When it comes to pouring the right liquids into your body, the most pervasive leadership challenge is moderating your alcohol consumption. I would say this is a discussion topic with at least one out of every five leaders I coach. Leaders, especially as they climb the ladder, justify excessive alcohol consumption with three primary reasons:

- **Others are doing it.** Alcohol is a staple at social events and client dinners. Often, there is unspoken pressure to participate—and continue to participate, especially if the leaders are the hosts who want everyone to have a good time.

- **I deserve it.** They believe they deserve an instant form of relaxation after a long workday.

- **I need it.** They use it to escape worrisome thoughts or troubling decisions that have held them captive all day.

The downside of excess is significant. Inevitably, you pay for it the next day. You are not fully present. You are not clear-headed. You are not light on your feet. You're either angry with yourself, ashamed of yourself, or afraid that others will figure out you had too much. And this assumes you didn't make a fool of yourself in front of others the night before.

If you routinely drink to excess because you are not going to work the next day, because it's the weekend or a holiday, the same negative factors can manifest themselves with your loved ones. You are not fully present for them—not present during the precious minority of your time that you spend with them. This isn't leading. This is running away, escaping, and numbing. All things in moderation.

Stay Fit

As you get older, your muscles do not naturally grow stronger. Your heart does not pump more efficiently. Your waist does not slim down gradually. And your limbs do not naturally become looser and more flexible. You know this. You know the exact opposite occurs. Your body, neglected a little or a lot, becomes heavier, softer, and less mobile. Working hard and running all over the place don't reverse any of this. In fact, they make things worse.

So you must lead yourself, just as you lead others. You must discipline yourself and hold yourself accountable. You must take care of this vehicle that enables you to show up at your best, as the leader.

You know what needs attention in your own body. Whether you have the self-discipline to do all this on your own or need the accountability of a personal trainer, classes, or group workouts, look at your calendar today and decide when you are going to start making physical fitness a priority.

I have worked with a CEO who makes fitness a priority in his life and in his company. On a monthly basis, most of his leadership team assembles in a different city for strategy and business development meetings. Each time, he arranges with the hotel to have a boot-camp-caliber fitness instructor lead the entire team in a one-hour workout, which is often followed by a second session for yoga. These monthly workouts alone will not get his senior team to their highest level of physical fitness, but they certainly serve as a powerful incentive for the executives to get and stay in shape in between. (Additionally, they tend to curb extended drinking sessions the night before!)

Another CEO found that swimming regularly was ideal for staying fit and managing stress. He enlisted his assistant to keep it a priority when he traveled. She learned to book him at hotels with or near a good pool for swimming laps.

Appearance is often the number-one motivator for staying physically fit. But for leaders, good looks alone won't cut it. When you are in good condition physically, your intellectual, emotional, and spiritual dimensions will be in better shape as well.

How you take care of your body is one measure of your ability to lead yourself. Most leaders know what they need to do. Some make excuses about why they can't. The disciplined ones just do it—consistently.

PHYSICAL SELF-LEADERSHIP CHALLENGE 2: ADDRESS STRESS NOW!

> ### 📝 "JOURNAL TIME"
>
> *Go to LeadLikeYouBook.com for an exercise related to this challenge.*

Twice in one month, I have sat in a conference room with grown men as they wept. Each of these men, one a president, the other a CIO, within minutes of sitting down with me, gave full physical expression to the stress they were experiencing. Two men, in different companies, each accomplishing everything put in front of them. Their common refrain? "Something has to change. I cannot keep going like this."

The closer you move to a top leadership position, the more susceptible you will be to stress. Leaders are vulnerable for two reasons in particular: the nonstop pace of life and social isolation. Many senior leaders don't even manage their own calendars anymore. They find themselves racing from meeting to meeting with barely enough time to go to the bathroom. And the old adage "It's lonely at the top" continues to be true. With whom can CEOs be vulnerable and discuss their greatest personal fears and worries?

Much of the experience of stress takes place in the physical dimension. And your body is equipped to respond to stress—in short bursts. It releases two hormones, adrenaline and cortisol, to deal with short-term threats. But when stress is continuous and activates these two fighters nonstop, day after day, your body will begin to break down, putting you at increased risk for the following:

- anxiety
- digestive problems
- sleep problems
- memory impairment
- depression
- heart disease
- weight gain
- difficulty concentrating

If any of these describe you, recognize that you are abusing your body.

> Continuous stress prevents you from leading like you were meant to.

In chapter 10, "Adjust," we'll address tactics for dealing with stress and reducing the havoc it can wreak on your body over time. For now, take inventory: Is your stress continuous? Are you starting to experience any of the symptoms listed above?

Your body is the vehicle for your leadership. To get better as a leader, become more aware of your presence, take better care of your body, listen to your gut instinct, and manage stress.

Although the physical dimension may be the foundational dimension of leadership, it is not the only dimension. Let's move on to the dimension many leaders tend to pride themselves on: the intellectual dimension.

KEY TAKEAWAYS

- To lead myself well in my physical dimension, I need to do three things:

    - understand how my physical presence speaks to others

    - be in good physical condition

    - learn to "listen" to my body through the signals it is trying to send me

- I can build awareness physically by tuning in to what my body is "saying" when I'm not speaking.

- When anticipating a big presentation or meeting, I need to pay as much attention to my physical preparation as I do to my mental preparation.

- I can manage my energy so I'm at my physical best for my most demanding leadership tasks.

- My body can sense danger and opportunity. It signals these to me through tensing muscles, breathing, and increasing heart rate, as well as the instinct to move away or toward others. If I listen

to my body, I may receive these signals sooner
than thinking or feeling them.

- My body is designed to handle temporary bouts
  of stress. It is not designed to handle stress on
  a continuous basis, which can compromise my
  leadership effectiveness.

QUESTIONS FOR REFLECTION

- Recall a time recently when you were present with others but not speaking. What might your physical presence have communicated to others?

- What is your ideal physical preparation to be at your best for a big presentation, conversation, or meeting?

- Reflect on a situation where you felt stressed or uncomfortable in the presence of others. Where did you feel that in your body? What did you feel like doing at that moment because of what you felt in your body?

- What are some changes you want to make in the next twenty-four hours to lead at your best physically?

- Go back to your Recent Regrettable Leadership Experience from chapter 2. What do you notice now about how you were showing up—physically?

- **Go to LeadLikeYouBook.com for additional exercises related to this chapter.**

CHAPTER 4

THE INTELLECTUAL DIMENSION

For as a person thinks, so are they.
— Proverbs 23:7

The mark of a certain kind of genius is the ability and energy to keep returning to the same task relentlessly, imaginatively, curiously, for a lifetime. Never give up and go on to something else; never get distracted and be diverted to something else. . . . Beethoven composed sixteen string quartets because he was never satisfied with what he had done. . . . Perfection eluded him—he kept coming back to it over and over in an attempt at mastery. . . . The same thing over and over, and yet it is never the same thing, for each venture is resplendent with dazzling creativity.
— Eugene Peterson, *Run with the Horses*

Recently, I sat down with a CEO. As usual, my opening question for him was "Tell me a story about you at your best or your worst during the past week." He immediately went to an incident he wasn't proud of but wanted to review with me.

Earlier that week, he had gone to the hospital to visit the family of an employee who was close to death. He was frustrated with the way he had interacted with the family members during the visit. He had failed at being a comfort or offering encouragement to them. He felt he could have prepared his remarks better. He left the ICU waiting room feeling a bit embarrassed and as if he had not encouraged the family in any way during his time with them.

So I had him replay the situation through the lens of each of the four dimensions. What was he aware of about himself during his visit—physically, intellectually, emotionally, and spiritually? When he came to the intellectual dimension, he said, "I remember thinking as I was getting out of my car, 'I don't want to be here.'"

Well, indeed. As he thought, so he was. Or wasn't!

Yes, he was there with the family physically—his body was in the room. But intellectually, was he present? No way. He was anywhere but there—because he wanted to be anywhere but there. And so as his body stood there, and his mouth opened, and the words started to come out, he fumbled and flailed and, in the end, made very little sense and said very little that he thought was comforting to the family. He wasn't prepared, because his mind was more preoccupied with the fact he didn't want to be at the hospital than with finding some appropriate words for this family in their time of grief. His mind was in a different place than his body. And it was on autopilot.

Knowing that this chapter is about increasing your awareness of your intellectual dimension, what is your reaction? You might be thinking, "Oh, I've got this," and maybe, "I can scan this chapter and move on to the next." Was I close?

The intellectual dimension of leaders is probably more familiar to us than any of the other three dimensions. That is because intellect gets a lot of attention on a daily basis. And it's been getting attention since we were very young—beginning with the first grades we received in school. The world routinely filters winners and losers according to intellect, to how smart a person is. After all, who doesn't want to hire, or serve under, a "smart" leader?

So it is no surprise that when I begin working with a leader, his or her self-awareness in the intellectual domain is sharper than in any of the other three dimensions, because we have been conditioned over decades to measure and improve our intellectual capacity. Look back at the notes you made about your Recent Regrettable Leadership Experience in chapter 2. How much of what you recorded reflects what you were thinking, or the logic you were applying, to that situation?

> My intellectual dimension may be sharpest because I've been conditioned my whole life to measure and improve it.

Besides believing we are already intellectually aware, we also tend to think that intellectual awareness is largely about how smart we are. Did I have the best suggestion in the staff meeting today? Did my boss like my answer more than everyone else's? Have I assembled the smartest team?

But intellectual awareness for leaders is about so much more than studies or smarts.

WHAT WERE YOU THINKING?!

Who was the last person who asked you this question—incredulity included? For me, it was probably my wife, Marta. She can do this because (a) as my wife, she feels she has the right to ask me that question, and (b) she has no hesitation challenging the logic of the words that come out of my mouth. Generally, if I can get past my automatic self-defensive response, I can ask myself the same question: "What *was* I thinking?!"

When it comes to thinking, we are like fish that don't realize they are swimming in water: we don't notice our thoughts, even though we swim in them all the time.

So this intellectual dimension is an area where we really should turn off the autopilot and grab the controls more often. As we swim along through our lives, we build up layer upon layer of automatic thinking that results in our minds just plowing ahead, never stopping to evaluate whether we are thinking the best thoughts in the best way possible. We may notice our immediate thoughts, but we fail to notice, and examine, the thoughts *behind* these thoughts.

> Like fish in water, we don't notice our thoughts, even though we swim in them all the time.

Lisa, who is president of a large real estate development firm, was disappointed with the way she had conducted herself during a property visit with her staff. When one of them criticized a team member in front of others, Lisa "erupted"—raising her voice and dressing down the first person who made the comment.

I had her replay the (regrettable) incident by looking at it through the four-dimensional lens—noticing what was going on inside her physically, intellectually, emotionally, and spiritually at the time. When she got to the intellectual dimension, she simply said, "I just didn't like what my first staff member said. I thought he was disrespectful to the other person." She then tried to move on to the emotional dimension.

I stopped her. "Wait. What else were you thinking?" As I got her to slow down and notice her "thoughts behind the thoughts," she eventually recognized three other important thoughts that had contributed to her losing her temper and behaving in a way she regretted:

- I'm generally deferential with my people.

- But from time to time, I need to remind them who is in charge.

- When I assert myself, I'm a jerk.

All of these thoughts contributed to Lisa, typically quiet and pleasant, finally deciding she was going to remind everyone who the boss was in a way that shocked her staff and caused her to regret her behavior. Indeed, if Lisa believes that when she asserts herself she's a jerk, she will probably behave like a jerk when she asserts herself. The light went on for Lisa when she realized these thoughts she rarely noticed—autopilot thoughts—had such a significant impact on her behavior.

So the first step to practicing intellectual self-awareness is to simply notice your thoughts. Another word for this is "mindfulness," which Dr. Daniel Siegel describes in this way:

> Mindfulness is a form of mental activity that
> trains the mind to become aware of awareness

itself and to pay attention to one's own intention. As researchers have defined it, mindfulness requires paying attention to the present
moment from a stance that is nonjudgmental
and nonreactive. It teaches self-observation;
practitioners are able to describe with words
the internal seascape of the mind. At the heart
of this process, I believe, is a form of internal
"tuning in" to oneself that enables people to
become "their own best friend."[9]

Before reading further, pause for a few minutes, and use
the list below to take inventory of all that is going on in your
head right now:

- **Volume of thoughts.** You have thousands of
  thoughts each day. Notice how many different
  things you are thinking about—simultaneously,
  even as you read this book: Thoughts about the
  room you are in. Thoughts about a work assign-
  ment. Thoughts about the people who are nearest
  to you. Thoughts about the morning's headlines.
  How are you doing juggling all those thoughts?

- **Thoughts about yourself.** Are you capable of
  doing the task in front of you? How are you judging yourself? When you think about your abilities,
  what do you think? Are you on top of things, or
  getting crushed? Are you confident, or are you
  questioning yourself?

- **Thoughts about others.** What do you think of
  others—your teammates, your competition, your
  boss, and your direct reports? Are you thinking

they are superior to you, or inferior? Are they
smart, or stupid? Do you admire them, or do they
just represent problems for you?

- **Aspirations and expectations.** What ideals are
  you holding on to—for yourself, for others, and
  for life? Where is your thinking filled with "ought-
  tos" and "shoulds"? What are the unspoken standards against which you are measuring yourself
  and others?

- **Past and future.** How many of your thoughts
  are devoted to the meeting or conversation you
  just left? How many to what you are scheduled to
  do next? How much are you still thinking about
  the blowup you had yesterday with your boss, or
  husband, or daughter? In short, how much of your
  thinking is in a time frame other than right now,
  the present?

- **Urges and impulses.** What thoughts are you having right now about eating something? Drinking
  something? Avoiding someone? Procrastinating?
  Leaving? Surfing? Ignoring? Texting?

Taking inventory of your thoughts is like taking inventory
of your company's products or services. You must know what
you have in order to best deploy or direct them. This is being
"mindful." If you did not notice any of your thoughts, this is
being "mindless."

📝 "JOURNAL TIME"

What did you notice? Record some of the highlights in your journal. Go to LeadLikeYouBook.com for a related exercise.

Do you notice multiple layers of thinking about the same issue—thoughts behind thoughts? Look at the stream of thoughts in this example from one of my leaders:

> *I need to finish my employee reviews today.*
> *Human Resources has been waiting for them.*
> *I want to be a good boss and give helpful feed-*
> *back to my people. Being a good leader means*
> *meeting deadlines. I need to set a good exam-*
> *ple. I should have done these at the beginning*
> *of the day when I wasn't thinking about so*
> *many other things. I don't think I have the time*
> *to do them today. I need to complete the sales*
> *proposal for our biggest customer. The rest of*
> *my sales team has done their jobs and now*
> *they are expecting me to do mine, today. I have*
> *no extra time tomorrow. I only have so much*
> *time. I'm going to swing by the break area and*
> *get a handful of peanut-butter pretzels. I still*
> *need to finish my employee reviews today. . . .*

In this example, we see all sorts of thoughts—thoughts about self; thoughts about others; aspirations for being a "good boss"; thoughts about yesterday, today, and tomorrow; and finally, the urge to procrastinate and eat a snack!

Some of these thoughts are conscious thoughts at the surface—like problem solving about when to complete multiple tasks. But many of them are subconscious—two or three layers underneath the surface—such as the ideals around what defines a "good boss" or the impulse to stop by the break room (table 1).

Conscious	Subconscious
THOUGHT	thought, thought, thought, thought, thought, thought, thought, thought, thought, thought, thought, thought
What I'm trying to think about or concentrate on	What I'm also thinking about

Table 1. Conscious and subconscious thoughts.

When you look at your recent inventory of all that is on your mind, which are the conscious thoughts, and which are the "thoughts underneath the thoughts"? As a leader, you would do well to notice what types of thinking you are engaged in, and how, when, and where you can do your best thinking.

THREE THINKING MODES

I remember having dinner at a bustling, crowded Italian restaurant in Manhattan one summer evening with a friend who had just taken over as executive producer of the nightly news for one of the major TV networks. As you might imagine, he felt a great deal of pressure in his new leadership role, and he was giving me a download of issues he had to navigate. Finally, in exasperation, he blurted out what so many other leaders feel when he said, "What I need more than anything right now is time to think!"

It struck me as ironic at that moment that he was saying this (actually, he was nearly shouting it) while he was in the middle of a busy, loud, jam-packed eatery in the middle of one of the busiest, loudest, most jam-packed cities in the world. What a metaphor for the thought life of leaders!

The reality, though, was that he had as much time as he needed to think. And he was thinking all the time. In fact, plenty of great, original, creative thinking goes on in New York City every day. The distinction I believe my friend was trying to make had more to do with the *type* of thinking he was engaged in. Whatever type of thinking it was, he was not getting enough of it.

Leaders have three modes of thinking available to them at any given time. Notice how each of these varies according to three variables: (a) the amount of *time* and *energy* it takes, (b) *the locus of control*, and (c) the role of *autopilot*:

- **Conscious thinking.** I begin with this one because it is the one we are most "conscious" of on a regular basis. Conscious thinking takes place in our brains' prefrontal cortex, which is far more developed in us than in the brains of animals. It's a big part of what makes us human. David Rock, a leading researcher on neuroscience and leadership, identifies five primary types of conscious thinking: understanding, deciding, recalling, memorizing, and inhibiting.[10] As leaders, we further combine these thinking modes for more complex tasks such as planning, problem solving, communicating, and other executive functions. In conscious thinking mode, we are in control of the thinking process, and much of our thinking is based on facts and information we already know, which are based on our education and experience. Conscious thinking certainly takes time, effort, and energy, but after a while, we grow weary of this mode of thinking and need to take a break.

Autopilot may or may not be turned on for conscious thinking.

- **Subconscious thinking.** Like a submarine cruising beneath the surface of the water, our subconscious mind does its work in stealth mode. Countless times each minute, it is evaluating, making decisions, adjusting to circumstances, and giving directions. I do not have to consciously turn it on or off. I don't need to schedule time for this mode of thinking. In fact, it takes so little energy and is so automatic, it is almost as if I am "not thinking." To this end, my subconscious thoughts can control me instead of me controlling them. Autopilot is fully engaged.

- **Creative thinking.** While subconscious thinking happens automatically and conscious thinking is an everyday necessity, creative thinking is required for leaders to create, innovate, and grow. The term "creative" doesn't just apply to artists or inventors. For leaders, creativity is the domain of solving big problems and thinking of new strategies. Leaders can intentionally and consciously think creative thoughts, but many "eureka moments" occur randomly and catch a leader by surprise. Creativity can take a lot of time, or a little, and a lot of energy, or a little. Perhaps the biggest distinction from the other two modes of thinking is that creative thinking requires leaders to let go of what they know and be curious—be "in the question." The reward is truly original thought with no autopilot.

Table 2 summarizes and compares these three modes of thinking.

Conscious	Subconscious	Creative
Focused; based on what I already know	Automatic, habitual; "not thinking"	Wandering, curious; based on what I know and don't know
Takes time	Takes no time	Ranges from instantaneous to taking a lot of time
Low volume of data[11]	Very high volume of data[12]	High volume of data; both conscious and subconscious
Average brain energy	Low brain energy	High brain energy
"I control my thoughts."	"My thoughts control me."	"I am open and curious, even though I have little or no control over my thoughts."
Proactive	Reactive	Proactive
Example: Carefully following directions to a new work location the first day	Example: Driving to work after one year without even thinking	Example: Imagining the benefits of working in a whole new office setting

Table 2. Conscious, subconscious, and creative thinking.

If you want to grow as a leader, and if you want to take on greater levels of responsibility, you must engage more of your creative thinking. Organizations look to their most senior leaders for innovation, new ideas, and better ways of doing things. If you are to provide this leadership, you must devote more time and energy to reflection and venture into the unknown.

LEADERS AND THEIR BRAINS: WHO'S IN CHARGE?

You won't innovate on autopilot. Let's remember that this chapter is about awareness in the intellectual dimension. You engage awareness so that you can disengage autopilot. Disengaging autopilot opens up the opportunity for you to think in new ways so that you, and those you lead, can be more creative and get new results.

> **If you want to grow as a leader and take on greater levels of responsibility, you must engage more creative thinking.**

If, when you read chapter 3, you became aware of aspects of your physical dimension that could be improved, you probably instinctively knew what you needed to do—for example, go to bed earlier for more sleep, hire a personal trainer to get in shape and lose weight, or change your eating or drinking habits.

> **You won't innovate on autopilot.**

Now, as you read this chapter, you may notice for the first time aspects of your intellectual dimension that could serve you better. Perhaps there's a lot of subconscious "chatter" in your head or a constant stream of negative thinking, or you have too little time devoted to vision, strategy, or other forms of creative thinking. The instinctive changes that came naturally for the physical dimension may not come as easily for the intellectual.

Fortunately, much progress has been made in recent years to help us understand how our brains work. In the past, motivational speakers exhorted us to "think positive thoughts" or "think outside the box" to think more creatively. But in recent years, neuroscientists have made great advances in understanding the concrete, observable activity occurring in our brain as we think. They have discovered that, just as we can exercise our bodies to be healthier, we actually have more control over our brain than previously known and can focus it in more productive directions. Think of this as self-leadership in the intellectual dimension.

New books and articles are being published daily about these wonderful discoveries in the field of neuroscience. Using these, along with over a decade of observing leaders as they think more effectively, I have identified four intellectual self-leadership challenges to help you manage your intellectual dimension, shift out of autopilot, and lead more effectively.

INTELLECTUAL SELF-LEADERSHIP CHALLENGE I: MANAGE YOUR BRAIN FUEL

"JOURNAL TIME"

Go to LeadLikeYouBook.com for an exercise related to this challenge.

I had a catch-up visit with a chief legal officer whom I had coached for a number of years, beginning when he first joined the company as a young attorney. We recalled how he used to work late into the night, either at the office or at home, reviewing legal documents. A couple of times in those days, I would see him toward the end of the business day, around 5:00 or 6:00 p.m., and he would already be zombielike from too little sleep the night before. And yet he would have ordered in dinner so as to spend another five to six hours reviewing legal filings.

He admitted to me that, more than once in those days, he would come in the next morning and take one last review of documents he had studied the night before—and catch multiple errors he had missed! It was a clear example of the results of a brain functioning on an empty tank at the end of the day versus a full tank in the morning!

Neuroscience explains this phenomenon. The brain may be an organ, but just like our muscles, it uses fuel to operate. And when that fuel is low, the brain doesn't operate so well.

Automatic subconscious thinking requires very little energy— analogous to the amount of brainpower you use to make the daily drive to a familiar location like work. But conscious thinking—the type you use as a leader for answering a client's email, developing a sales campaign, preparing a speech, or finalizing contracts—burns a lot of energy, sucking up metabolic fuel in your bloodstream. The more tired our brains get, the harder we try to focus—which only burns our intellectual fuel even faster.[13]

You can deceive yourself by reasoning, as my attorney friend did, that at 10:00 p.m., "I'm still awake, I'm still at work, and therefore I should still be able to concentrate on this presentation deck for tomorrow's meeting." But generally, the lights are on but nobody's home—nobody, at least, who is at his or her best for planning and decision making.

Staying constantly "connected" to catch the latest email or text is also a major brain drain. It is like plugging your phone in to recharge but then unplugging it every time you have an incoming message or phone call. You are draining the battery and stretching out the time it will take to replenish and get back to full strength.

Here are six recommendations for self-leadership in managing your brain's energy:

- Focus on one problem at a time.

- Subdivide larger problems into smaller problems.

- Prioritize those tasks that require conscious thinking energy (e.g. emails and texts ping us for attention, but they are probably secondary to bigger tasks).

- Recognize when your brain energy is low, push back from the task, and replenish (even overnight) before attacking it again.

- Schedule your time for different modes of thinking that require different amounts of energy.

- Disconnect from technology for distinct periods every day or week.

Being aware of your brain's energy level for leadership tasks leads us to the next intellectual challenge.

INTELLECTUAL SELF-LEADERSHIP CHALLENGE 2: NOTICE AND MINIMIZE YOUR ASSUMPTIONS

> ✍ **"JOURNAL TIME"**
>
> *Go to LeadLikeYouBook.com for an exercise related to this challenge.*

One of the big dangers of being on autopilot is that you are not fully in charge. When autopilot is on, your instincts and feelings take over, dictating your behavior. The same goes for your thoughts. If you are not careful, your autopilot thinking will lead you into dangerous territory.

As I said in the first intellectual self-leadership challenge earlier, a healthy brain is very energy efficient. When it comes to problem solving, your brain's default is to use less fuel by focusing more on the known than on the unknown.[14] Leaders are particularly vulnerable here because they constantly feel pressure to know the facts, to know the solution, and to have answers.

When running on autopilot, leaders' brains can take shortcuts by signaling the leader that "you already have this person or this problem figured out." One big way the brain takes shortcuts to certainty is with assumptions—made-up stories. I witness assumptions tripping up leaders all the time. Within one week, I heard these statements from leaders:

- "He doesn't want our team to be successful."

- "She is never open to any of our ideas."

- "He's just goofing off when he's not in the office."

It's always interesting to notice the certainty with which leaders will make these statements. When I hear them, they make me want to ask, "Do you know for a fact that is true?" "Did she tell you she doesn't want to hear any new ideas?" "Have you observed him goofing off?"

When we are on autopilot, we like to make up these assumptions so we can have an answer to "explain things." Here's the hidden trap for leaders who let their brains be in charge: The brain doesn't care if the assumption is correct or not, it just wants to have an answer. Once it has an explanation for why something happened or why someone did something the way they did, the brain is ready to move on to its next problem to solve.

And so leaders take questionable assumptions and make them the foundation on which they build their plan of action, their solution to a problem, or their negative feedback to a subordinate.

Curiosity is the healthy antidote to autopilot assumptions. Curiosity prompts the leader to double-check his or her assumptions or to just ask the question outright. Take the examples of assumptions I listed previously. I'll restate the assumption and then the more helpful curiosity question:

Assumption says, "He doesn't want our team to be successful."

Curiosity asks, "What are your goals for our team?"

Assumption says, "She is never open to any of our ideas."

Curiosity asks, "We have some ideas. Could we share them with you?"

Assumption says, "He's just goofing off when he's not in the office."

Curiosity asks, "How did you spend your time yesterday?"

A leader's assumption is generally based on past experience. So he or she often has some basis for holding that assumption. But far too often, leaders can steer a more accurate course by first questioning or confirming their assumptions.

The leader's curious question may well simply confirm the assumption was accurate. But genuine curiosity often opens up new ways of thinking for everyone.[15] Remember, your brain likes to be lazy by assuming it already "knows." Intellectual self-leadership expends the extra energy needed for curiosity and new learning.

> ## Curiosity is the healthy antidote to autopilot assumptions.

INTELLECTUAL SELF-LEADERSHIP CHALLENGE 3: MANAGE YOUR THOUGHTS SO THEY DON'T MANAGE YOU!

📓 "JOURNAL TIME"

Go to LeadLikeYouBook.com for an exercise related to this challenge.

One other aspect of managing your intellectual dimension is to be selective in what thoughts you choose to think. The leader's brain on autopilot is like an airport with no security checkpoint. With no checkpoint, anyone is allowed to get on the airplane, including bad guys. Similarly, autopilot for the leader allows just any thought to enter his or her mind, even if that thought is not helpful or, worse, even true.

Go back to the inventory of thoughts you did earlier in this chapter, in the "What Were You Thinking?!" section. Which of the thoughts are true, and which are not true? Which are helpful, and which are not helpful?

When I get on coaching calls with leaders who are struggling, we will do a four-dimensional inventory, and often, when we get to their intellectual dimension, they will notice they are having thoughts like "This problem is impossible to solve," "I'm an imposter, and they just don't know it," or "If I don't ace this presentation, they might fire me."

> You have your thoughts; your thoughts don't have to have you.

I then ask them, "Is that a helpful thought or not?" Pretty quickly they discern the helpful from the unhelpful thoughts. I remind them they are in a position to choose their thoughts and to select the ones that are useful. Often, I'll take them a step further and ask them, "Is it possible there are other thoughts out there that could be helpful as well?" This question nudges the lazy brain to explore other possibilities rather than just default back to a known problem.

One useful visual concept is to see your thoughts as a series of packages on a conveyor belt. This concept helps create a little distance between you and your thoughts. Often, we view ourselves as the sum of our thoughts. But here, we see that we can stand independently of our thoughts. Put another way, you have your thoughts; your thoughts don't have to have you.

Figure 5. When you are aware, you can choose to keep helpful thoughts and let go of thoughts that are not helpful.

Secondly, this visual puts you in charge of your thoughts. You are in the position of choosing which thought packages you are going to pick up and which ones you are just going to let go on down the conveyor belt. Thoughts marked "harmful," "negative," "dangerous," or "false"—we just let those thoughts keep going. And instead, we pick up the thoughts labeled "useful," "interesting," "true," and "helpful."

I'm not merely advocating the age-old notion of "positive thinking" here. Leaders need a balance of realistic and objective thought to make good decisions. But the key is that leaders stay in charge, which includes managing their thoughts.

INTELLECTUAL SELF-LEADERSHIP CHALLENGE 4: CHANGE HOW YOU THINK

📝 **"JOURNAL TIME"**

Go to LeadLikeYouBook.com for an exercise related to this challenge.

David Rock, a leading researcher on the relationship between neuroscience and leadership, says, "It is attention itself that changes the brain."[16] The more you notice your thoughts, the more you can change how you think. Change how you think, and you can change how you lead.

> The more you notice your thoughts, the more you can change how you think. Change how you think, and you can change how you lead.

Your brain thinks in maps. Consider the starting point a problem or question, and the end point a solution or answer. Connecting the starting and end points is something called a neural pathway, a circuit of connected neurons.[17] The very first time you have a new thought, your brain is forcing itself to connect neurons and blaze a path from point A to point B (figure 6). Just so you can sound savvy with your friends, this process can be summed up in the statement "Neurons that fire together, wire together."

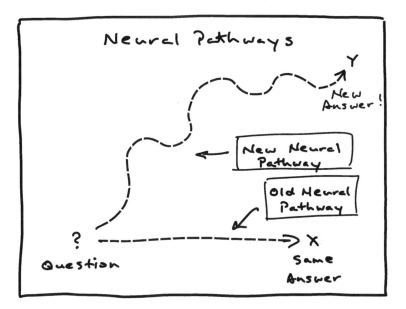

Figure 6. Old neural pathways vs. new neural pathways.

But it is hard for the brain to make these connections the first time. Think of how hard it would be to blaze a one-mile trail connecting two villages deep in the Amazon. I picture a lot of sweat, and probably some blood and tears—so much so that you might be tempted to give up and return to the first village rather than persevere to your destination. But imagine if you persisted, kept your eye on the prize, and finally broke through the brush into the clearing of the second village.

And instead of just navigating the trail once, each day thereafter you kept walking that trail back and forth, some days multiple times. Each time you walked it, you made it a little wider, a little more established. After months or years of walking that trail, there would be nothing but dirt under your feet. In contrast to the hard work and energy it took to blaze the trail the first time, now it's a delight to take this path. You could almost walk it with your eyes closed.

Let's be explicit about the lessons from this trailblazing illustration, because they apply to your thinking (and those you lead!) as well:

- Blazing the trail the first time is hard work and requires a lot of energy and focus on the destination.

- Walking the trail the second and third times still requires a lot of effort.

- The more you walk the trail, the easier it becomes.

- With enough repetition, walking the trail becomes second nature.

The same applies when you accept my challenge to change how you think about a particular topic:

- A new thought, supported by curiosity, takes a lot of concentration.

- Continuing with the new thought requires intention and repetition.

- Gradually, as you repeat the way of thinking, it becomes easier.

- Eventually, thinking this new way becomes second nature.

Often, a leader will say to me, "That's just the way I am." And when I hear that, I always encourage them to add three magical words: "up until now." This is because our brains are not hardwired.

Regardless of how we feel at times, especially stressful times, we are not just "stuck" with ourselves as we currently are. We do have the ability to create new mind maps and to think differently. And, as we will discuss later, thinking differently enables behaving differently, which leads to new outcomes.

Now that you have tools to better notice and manage your thoughts, let's turn to the risky, scary, uncomfortable, sometimes awkward emotional dimension. Yes, we're going to talk about leaders and feelings!

KEY TAKEAWAYS

- I have thoughts. My thoughts don't need to have me. But they will have me—they will be in charge—if I am on autopilot.

- "Mindfulness" is not some mystical activity reserved for meditation or silent retreats. It is the intentional practice of pausing to notice my thoughts—all of them.

- I have three different modes of thinking:

  - conscious thoughts

  - subconscious thoughts

  - creative thoughts

- Just as the muscles in my body need fuel or energy to function, so my brain relies on fuel for thinking. I would do well to manage my brain fuel so plenty is available for my best, most creative thinking.

- Because I don't always have complete information, I use assumptions to fill the gaps. I need to remember that my assumptions are rarely 100 percent correct. I need to look for opportunities to ask curious questions to get more facts and reduce my use of assumptions for decision making and problem solving.

- When I turn off autopilot and notice my thoughts, I am in a better position to manage my thoughts rather than let them manage me.

- Rather than surrendering with "that's just who I am," I can intentionally decide to think in new ways that open up the possibility to show up and lead in new ways.

- Just as thinking the way I've always thought has come through repetition, so I will need the benefit of time and repetition to think in new ways.

QUESTIONS FOR REFLECTION

- What are some recent examples where you were thinking on autopilot?

- When does thinking on autopilot help your leadership? When does autopilot thinking degrade your leadership?

- How do you currently manage yourself to do your best, most creative thinking as a leader?

- Overall, what changes do you need to make to better manage your intellectual dimension?

- Go back to your Recent Regrettable Leadership Experience from chapter 2. What do you notice now about how you were showing up—intellectually?

- **Go to LeadLikeYouBook.com for additional exercises related to this chapter.**

CHAPTER 5

THE EMOTIONAL DIMENSION

The governing factor . . . was motion—keep moving; under no circumstances stay still and feel the feelings. That would have been unbearable.
  —Eric Clapton, *Clapton: The Autobiography*

I have learned now that while those who speak about one's miseries usually hurt, those who keep silence hurt more.
  —C. S. Lewis

A little over twenty years ago, I was sitting at Clyde's, a restaurant in Chevy Chase, Maryland, having lunch with one of my best friends. I had known this friend since college. And on this day, after a couple of decades of doing life together, he had a message for me: "Rob, you need to spend less time in your head and more time in your heart."

I recall being so puzzled. I had always considered myself "sensitive"—especially as a man. And though I felt safe with this longtime friend, I also felt defensive in response to his statement. I kept asking him to clarify what he meant. "Why are you saying that?" "How do I do this?" I was, of course, try-ing to use my brain to help me connect with my heart!

Well, I didn't learn fully what he meant that day, and it actually took me another ten-plus years and a lot of work to start connecting with my heart and feeling my feelings. In the decade that followed, I learned to pause, turn off autopilot, and notice my emotional state. By becoming more aware of my feelings—*feeling* my feelings—I began to recognize the power-ful influence my emotions have on my other three dimensions and how they influence so much of how I show up and behave.

My wife, Marta, who has been with me for over thirty years, would tell you that I have made some progress. And yet I am still working at it.

In the last two chapters, we have learned about the two dimensions that, frankly, come easiest to most of us. Physically, we have become better attuned to how we carry ourselves, the message our faces send, our breathing, where we carry our tension, and the care and feeding of our bodies. Intellectually, we now understand we are more than just what we learned in school. We have become more aware of the subconscious thoughts underneath the conscious thoughts, and we recog-nize that some of our thoughts need to be reexamined. Indeed, we've learned that, with intention and repetition, we can change the way we think.

Now we turn to more challenging territory. In this chap-ter, we will move to becoming more self-aware emotionally, a dimension we often try to hide from others and that can even remain hidden from ourselves. Indeed, from the vantage points of those around us, our emotions can be the tip of an iceberg, where we reveal only a little bit on the surface, but underneath, there is a lot more going on. We can smile on the outside while feeling great sadness or pain on the inside.

As leaders, we must become more aware emotionally, because our emotions absolutely influence our behavior. And our behavior dictates our results. If we want different results and different behavior, we have to become aware of how our emotions influence us and how they impact those we lead.

I will never forget sitting in an airline lounge at LaGuardia Airport introducing the four dimensions to a leader named Edward. Edward had recently been named "Engineer of the Year" by a large Silicon Valley firm. This company asked me to coach Edward because they were concerned he was no longer motivated and might leave them to pursue greater career challenges with a competitor.

So at our first meeting, I walked Edward through the importance of being self-aware as a beginning point for leadership change. I described the physical and intellectual dimensions. He nodded, tracking with me. But as I began to describe emotional self-awareness, I noticed him shift in his seat, his face going taut and his eyebrows furrowing. Suddenly, he couldn't keep quiet any longer and blurted out harshly, "This is b---s---! Emotions have nothing to do with the workplace! It's all about the bottom line!"

I was taken aback. I had never experienced such a reaction from a new client. Pausing, I had to think fast about how to respond. Clearly, he was feeling an emotion—anger. Then I slowly noticed my own emotional response to his angry outburst. I noticed that I was afraid.

Here I was, trying to teach a leader some foundational principles as our coaching relationship was forming, and he was rejecting me! How would we build a trusting, productive partnership if he refused to entertain this new paradigm for seeing himself? I felt cold beads of sweat trickling down the sides of my torso, but I tried to not let my anxiety show.

In that split-second pause to consider what I would say next, I noticed my fear, and I realized I had a choice in how to respond. Option A was to be led by my fear and stop trying to introduce my four-dimensional framework. Option B was to press on courageously. I chose option B: "I hear you and understand you see it that way, but I'd like you to hang with me a little longer as we explore this dimension together." I finished introducing him to the four dimensions.

The whole exchange with Edward illustrated the very point I was introducing to him. Emotions are always present—in the workplace and everywhere else. And they absolutely impact our behavior and results. If Edward had been my boss, I might have reacted to his outburst by shutting down out of fear and not risk telling him everything I thought he ought to know about an issue. If I had been his boss, my anger might have led me to write him up or curtail his responsibilities.

Fortunately, I soldiered on with Edward, and the interesting ending to his story is that, when he finally connected with his emotions, he experienced a tremendous breakthrough professionally. Over the next six months, using the principles of becoming a four-dimensional leader that I outline in this book, Edward discovered his passions—what made him truly happy and alive. And out of that discovery, he proceeded to create a new position at his firm in which he could drive significant new sales for the company while doing the job he really wanted to do.

WE ARE ALL EMOTIONAL

We are all emotional beings. I like to say that we all came wired from the factory with emotions. In fact, emotions were our first means of communicating with those around us. We were feeling, and letting others know how we felt, from the moment we were born. Anyone who has had children, or has been around babies recently, will immediately recognize how true this is. And it was true of you.

From the opening minutes of your life, you were letting your mother know whether you were happy or mad. You were upset when you first had to leave the warm, comfortable confines of your mother's womb. And you conveyed this anger as you cried and the doctor cut your umbilical cord.

But then you were swaddled and hugged and given some milk, and you were happy. And you communicated this happiness to those around you by being peaceful in your body, maybe even audibly cooing.

Then, when you were awakened suddenly or wanted your diaper changed, you got angry and let the outside world know by pitching a little fit. Think about how much you were feeling emotions and communicating with emotions in the opening hours of your life!

As time went by and you began to be aware that things like toys or a pacifier might be given to you and then taken away, you felt the emotion of sadness.

Eventually, one day, when your parents weren't hovering over you and guarding your every move, something surprised and frightened you. And you felt fear for the first time.

You felt all these feelings, and communicated them, long before you could even say your first words—long before anyone could even teach you about them. You felt them, and you used those feelings, because they were as much a part of you as your fingers and your toes. You have been "emotional" from the beginning of your life!

But one day something unfortunate happened, either in a big way, or a little way. It was different for all of us. You started to learn that there was something wrong with feeling feelings or with expressing them. And the wiring you had from the factory got rewired!

HOW "BEING EMOTIONAL" GOT DISTORTED

So how did we get here? How did we get to the place where Edward at LaGuardia was the first time I met him and where many leaders are now, believing that emotions don't belong in the workplace, much less in a discussion about being a better leader? I can't untangle the sequencing for all of us, but somewhere, likely in the first two decades of our lives, we began to receive some distorted messages about emotions. Generally speaking, these distorted messages brought us to one of three conclusions:

1. **"Don't feel."** Some of us were told to shut down our hearts at an early age with the message "don't cry" or "don't be angry."[18] Or we might have suffered trauma or neglect from a parent or authority figure whom we expected to love and protect us. How about this feedback from an authority figure: "You should be ashamed of yourself!" Such messages or experiences caused so much pain that they resulted in us numbing ourselves and not feeling our feelings.

2. **"Don't let your feelings show."** This variation might have given room for having feelings but being told not to express them. "Big boys don't cry" is one for the ages, as well as "If you're going to be angry, go to your room," "Don't be scared," and "Don't get so excited." The truth is, even when we try to hide our feelings, it shows through to others in the form of rigidity and stiffness. We do our best to push our feelings down and not express them with our bodies or with our words, but eventually they leak out.

3. **"Awkward!"** From the playground of our childhood to the office of our adulthood, there are people standing over in the corner gossiping about or
   mocking those that express their emotions. Many
   adults today are still children when it comes to
   experiencing sadness, fear, anger, and even joy—in
   themselves or in others. "Mike has an anger issue"
   or "She is just so emotional" can be messages that
   convey something is wrong with us if we share on
   the outside what we are feeling on the inside.

Whatever the reason, many of us find emotions difficult
to handle—whether our own or others'. But self-leadership,
and being at our best as a leader, requires that we master this
dimension, not try to ignore it or pretend it doesn't exist.

DEVELOPING YOUR EMOTIONAL VOCABULARY

When I first help leaders recognize their emotions, I ask them,
"What are you feeling right now?"

And so I ask that question of you. Pause reading for a
moment, and consider your emotional dimension right now.
What is one word you would use to describe how you are
feeling?

Right now, I am feeling _____.

Leaders generally respond in one of three ways when I
ask this question of them the first time. Most often, they will
quickly respond with "I'm okay," as if to say, "Can we move
on? I'm uncomfortable with this topic." Or there will be a long
pause, followed by an honest "I don't know." Or finally, they
say, "Well, I think that I am . . . ," in which case they intellectu-
alize their emotions. (If you didn't catch that, notice the word
"think" in response to the question about feelings.)

So early on, I help leaders relearn their emotional vocabulary. You have a lot of words you can use to express feelings, but the vast majority of them will fall under one of the following five: glad, sad, mad, scared, and ashamed. Four of these were in our original wiring. The fifth one "happened" to us.

Four Primary Emotions: Glad, Sad, Mad, and Scared

These four are called "primary" because all of us come hardwired with them as babies. And we all continue to possess and feel one or more of these emotions at different intensity levels all the time.

Depending on our circumstances and stress levels, we feel them in varying degrees of intensity. For instance, you may not feel "glad" at the moment, but you may feel "content"—a low level of "glad." Think of each primary emotion as having a range of intensity, like a volume knob, from low to high (table 3).

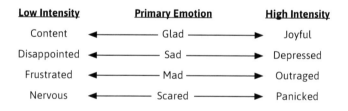

Low Intensity	Primary Emotion	High Intensity
Content	⟵——— Glad ———⟶	Joyful
Disappointed	⟵——— Sad ———⟶	Depressed
Frustrated	⟵——— Mad ———⟶	Outraged
Nervous	⟵——— Scared ———⟶	Panicked

Table 3. Each emotion has a "volume knob" ranging from low to high.

Try this. Take a moment to consider the word you used earlier to fill in the statement about how you are feeling right now. Which of the four primary emotions does that word fall under?

Now, the value of being able to name your emotion really goes up when you define what the emotion means. Each of these four primary emotions can be defined according to the relationship between "me" and "what I want":

- I feel glad. = I *have* what I want.

- I feel mad. = There is a *barrier* between me and what I want.

- I feel sad. = What I want *has been taken away* from me.

- I feel scared. = What I want *could be taken away* from me.

Notice that we are taking something that can seem either overwhelming or vague and beginning to break it down into smaller pieces. Like solving a big problem by breaking it down into smaller problems, our emotion becomes easier to understand, and thus easier for us to control rather than let it control us.

Consider your present feeling and its object ("what I want"). How does this help you better understand what you are feeling and why? Some of us can find it difficult to acknowledge "what I want," as if we are not worthy, need to ask permission, or are being overly selfish with our personal preferences or desires. But by clarifying what you want, you reveal an unspoken desire. Like the emotion itself, this desire might have even been hidden from you.

Feeling mad also presents us with the additional element of a barrier. Besides naming "what I want," name the barrier as well.

Notice that each of these four primary emotions is associated with a different point in time. Glad and mad are right now, in the present. Sadness pertains to the past, something I used to have. And scared is connected with the future. Whether seconds away or years away, it hasn't happened yet—but it could! I call fear an "emotion of the head," because in order to feel scared, we have to use our brains to imagine what could happen.

Mom's Mood

❍ Super	❍ Good	❍ Okay	❍ Bad	❍ Watch Out

Figure 7. A sign that hangs in the McKinnon kitchen.

A Learned Emotion: Shame

Whether or not shame is a natural part of our hard wiring is debatable. No baby feels ashamed all on his or her own. We feel shame as a result of what another person has said or done to us. One of the best ways to understand shame is by distinguishing between guilt and shame:

Guilt says, "I have *done something* wrong."

Shame says, "There *is something wrong* with me."

There is a big difference between feeling bad about my actions and feeling bad about who I am. One criticizes my behavior; the other strikes at my core and diminishes my worth.

"Shame" is a strong word—not one we hear people use every day. It generally reveals itself in more subtle ways:

- "If I could land that job, my dad would finally be proud of me."
- "If I could get that promotion and make the money that comes with it, then we could move into a new neighborhood . . . buy a new car . . .

get our kids into that private school . . . and my
friends would finally respect me."

- "If I don't receive that industry achievement
  award, I'll be shattered."

The original source of what happened that makes a person feel shame varies. For some, it could be something rather
benign—like being rejected by certain groups or cliques
when growing up, or being teased about the house their family lives in.

For others, it was a more traumatic form of abuse—
verbal, physical, emotional, or sexual. The deeper the wound
from these forms of trauma, the more likely one could benefit
from professional counseling or therapy.

> **Many leaders are driven by a sense of shame.**

Whatever the origin, I would say that nearly half of the
senior leaders I work with—CEOs, presidents, and C-suite
occupants—are driven, and have been driven, by a sense of
shame. These are high-performing leaders who have accomplished a lot. Because they struggle deep down with a sense
of unworthiness, it is critically important that they prove to
others that they *are* worthy. It is as if they have spent their lives
trying to outrun shame.

You now have a more robust vocabulary to name your
emotions. By naming your emotions, you have power over
them and can use them as a leader to problem solve. All of this
pertains to the inner game of leadership—you leading yourself.

Once again, let's pause our autopilot and become more aware of our emotional dimension. Here are three ways you can harness your emotional dimension to more powerfully lead and influence others.

EMOTIONAL SELF-LEADERSHIP CHALLENGE I: NOTICE AND MANAGE YOUR EMOTIONS

📝 **"JOURNAL TIME"**

Go to LeadLikeYouBook.com for an exercise related to this challenge.

Your emotions are not intrinsically good or bad. It's easy to label a feeling other than "glad" as bad or inappropriate. But the other emotions have their place too. It is appropriate to feel angry if we witness an injustice, to feel fear when danger threatens, or to feel sad if we have lost someone we love. All the emotions have their place.

Here is the distinction I make with leaders about emotions:

- Emotions are helpful when you recognize them and then manage them (lead yourself).

- Emotions are dangerous when you fail to recognize them (because you are on autopilot) and they manage you!

Emotions are like warning lights on your leadership dashboard—signals to "pay attention!" If you don't pay attention, either by willfully trying to ignore them or by mindlessly being on autopilot, your emotions will be in charge. And they will influence your behavior in a way that sabotages your leadership.

But if you pause and are aware, you can manage them and lead yourself to have a more intentional and resourceful response to the situation. For instance, not noticing how angry I am could result in me losing my temper, lashing out, and saying something I will regret. Noticing my anger enables me to pause, identify what I think is wrong that I want to be right, and pursue a constructive path in that direction.

Not noticing my fear could result in me saying "no" to a new opportunity offered to me because I don't feel prepared and fear failing. But turning off autopilot and noticing my fear could lead to me opening the door to the new opportunity while looking specifically at how I need to prepare to take it on.

EMOTIONAL SELF-LEADERSHIP CHALLENGE 2: USE YOUR EMOTIONS TO SOLVE PROBLEMS AND MAKE DECISIONS

> ### "JOURNAL TIME"
>
> *Go to LeadLikeYouBook.com for an exercise related to this challenge.*

When I first challenge leaders to notice their emotions, I emphasize that I am not advocating they connect with their feelings just so they can be more of a "touchy-feely" leader. No! When you learn to recognize your emotions, you will find they can help you in the day-to-day leadership challenges of problem solving and decision making.

To see how this works, let's take a look at three steps that transform our feelings into helpful leadership tools.

- **Step 1.** Name the feeling. For example, "I am worried that I won't complete the acquisition report on time." The feeling is "worry."

- **Step 2.** Associate that feeling with one of the four primary emotions. For example, "Worry is a form of fear."

- **Step 3.** Use the definition of the emotion to clarify what I want. For example, "What do I want that could be taken away from me? I want to be viewed as capable of doing this work. I want to continue to be in charge of this project. I fear my authority could be taken away if this report doesn't send the message that I am capable of being in charge."

> ## Emotions can help you with making big decisions and solving big problems.

Simply naming the emotion and getting to the root of what it is trying to tell you reduces the (usually negative) energy it can have over you. That's good.

But here's what's even better. Knowing the emotion you are feeling brings clarity to a problem you are trying to solve, or a decision you are trying to make, in that it helps you identify what it is you ultimately want. This enables you to be focused in your actions and clear in your communication with others. Instead of wasting energy in an emotional wrestling match with yourself, you can concentrate on pursuing what it is you want to get done.

By the way, I find in my work with leaders (and myself!) that we don't pause often enough to clarify what exactly we want. Emotions provide a helpful reminder to stop and respond to this question.

> ## A big question for leaders is "What exactly do I want?"

EMOTIONAL SELF-LEADERSHIP CHALLENGE 3: LEAD POWERFULLY BY CONNECTING WITH YOUR HEART

> ### 🖊 "JOURNAL TIME"
>
> *Go to LeadLikeYouBook.com for an exercise related to this challenge.*

Our goal as leaders is to not just be able to name our feelings but to feel our feelings. When we can do that, we will lead ourselves better and lead others better. Only by connecting with our own heart can we genuinely connect with the hearts of those we lead.

I once coached a candidate running for public office. This leader, who had been quite successful in business, was very smart. An engineer by training, he had some well-thought-out solutions to some of the biggest problems facing his community. And yet, when he spoke, the crowd would respond with polite applause and little enthusiasm. His campaign had big ideas but little energy.

As I worked with him on being more self-aware, he began to realize that he was off balance in the four dimensions, especially between his head and his heart. As he described to me a key point he wanted to make in an upcoming speech, he talked at length about how thoroughly he had thought the issue through and why his logic made sense.

Finally, having heard enough from his head, I asked him how his heart felt about the issue. Without hesitation, out of his mouth came the words "Well, here's why I care about this issue so much. . . ." With that, he went back to an experience from his childhood that was the basis for why he had so much passion for solving this particular problem. He got out of his head and into his heart.

Those words—"here's why I care about this issue so much"—became the connecting statement between his head and his heart for the campaign. Whether he was in a debate with the other candidates or speaking in front of the Jaycees, he would make a point (intellectual), then he would pivot and say, "and here's why I care so much about this," and go on to describe his own (emotional) feeling about the issue.

The first time he tried this, he had a fellow come up to him afterward and say, "I'm not from your party, but I plan to vote for you!" From that point forward, he saw a new level of engagement in the faces of his audience, and the applause was more enthusiastic. He was connecting with people's hearts.

There is a term for this phenomenon: emotional contagion. As the term implies, emotions are contagious—people will mimic and synchronize their personal emotions with the emotions expressed by others around them.

You want followers who follow you because they want to, not because they have to. "Want" comes from the heart. And the best way to awaken that want in the hearts of those you lead is to connect with their hearts—from your heart.[19]

Your emotions impact your behavior, as well as the behavior of those around you. The more senior you are, and the more emotionally expressive, the greater your impact. Emotionally self-aware leaders channel their emotions constructively to influence and motivate the behavior of their followers. Emotionally detached leaders not only detach from themselves but from their people as well, leading to dysfunction. Leaders who are not emotionally self-aware will build walls, not trust.

Think about a leader from your past who inspired you and who elicited the best that you had to offer. What was it about this leader that engaged you so? Pause, say the person's name out loud to yourself, and then think of the ways this leader inspired you.

I'm betting that one of the key things you remember about this person was that he or she connected with your heart in some way. Yes, he or she may have been really smart, or simply wise through years of experience. But what makes this leader stand out from other good leaders you have known was his or her emotional presence.

> Leaders who are not emotionally self-aware will build walls, not trust.

Your leadership advances to a whole new dimension when you connect with and activate the emotions of those you are trying to lead. The saying "People don't care how much you know until they know how much you care" rings true here.

As I've observed in my years of working with leaders and know from experience, it takes time and intentional practice to become more self-aware of our emotions. Don't expect one chapter of this book to make you a pro overnight. But just as we have learned with the physical and intellectual dimensions, the more you exercise this emotional muscle, the stronger it becomes. Start noticing your emotions and how they affect your behavior. Like the leaders I work with each day, you will lead yourself better, begin adjusting your behavior, and get new results!

We've now addressed the three leadership dimensions—physical, intellectual, and emotional—that are most easily seen by others. Now let's turn our awareness to the more mysterious part of ourselves that lies underneath—our spiritual dimension.

KEY TAKEAWAYS

- My behavior dictates my results. My emotions influence my behavior. If I want different results, I need to notice my emotions and how they influence my behavior.

- I am an emotional being. I was born hardwired with emotions.

- As I grew up, different people and influences probably changed my understanding of my emotions, especially the influence they can have on me as a leader.

- I was born with four primary emotions: glad, sad, mad, and scared. Another emotion I probably learned along the way is shame. Each of these emotions can be defined as the relationship between "me" and "what I want."

- Emotions themselves are not good or bad. What is good or bad is whether I am noticing and managing them (good) or they are managing me (bad). My emotions will manage me if I am on autopilot.

- As a leader, connecting with my emotions is not about getting more touchy-feely! By tuning in to my emotions, I am better equipped to solve problems and make decisions constructively.

- To really have influence with others, I need to connect with their hearts. I can only connect with their hearts by way of my heart.

QUESTIONS FOR REFLECTION

- What people or experiences shaped or influenced your emotions as you grew up?

- Recall a time when you were on autopilot and your emotions were "in charge" of you. What did you want in that situation?

- What emotion(s) do you notice most often in yourself? Do you let others see this emotion or do you try to cover it up?

- When you are at your best as a leader, how are you self-leading your emotional dimension?

- What are one or two changes you want to make as a leader in your emotional dimension?

- Go back to your Recent Regrettable Leadership Experience from chapter 2. What do you notice now about how you were showing up—emotionally?

- **Go to LeadLikeYouBook.com for additional exercises related to this chapter.**

CHAPTER 6
THE SPIRITUAL DIMENSION

Who am I?

—Jean Valjean, *Les Misérables*

The two most important days in your life are the day you are born and the day you find out why.

—Original author unknown

"I'm just so tired of feeling ashamed all the time."

It's not often someone confesses "feeling ashamed" in your first conversation together.

I was driving down the interstate, south of Washington DC, and was having an introductory call with a leader who had been referred to me for coaching. Brian led a major division of a public company. We had been chatting, getting to know one another for about forty-five minutes, when I finally asked him, "So why, exactly, are we talking today?" With barely a pause, he answered, describing this hidden burden of shame.

This was a guy who, as far as I could tell, had had a pretty successful run. He had garnered industry awards, started and sold several companies, and now was working for the firm that bought his last company. He continued: "I'm tired of always worrying about what others are thinking of me and my performance."

I knew we had touched something deep. Before even starting our work together, he had already identified a key issue, something that went deeper than just his feeling of shame and penetrated to the very core of who he was—his identity. And regardless of all his outward signs of success and having it together as a leader, it was an inner burden that he carried every day.

Over the past three chapters, we have slowly journeyed inward, building awareness of how we—our bodies, our thoughts, and our feelings—show up as leaders. We have moved from noticing what is more obvious to others and to ourselves, to what is more concealed from others—and ourselves.

As we sharpen our awareness of what is going on in our physical, intellectual, and emotional dimensions, we become better at leading ourselves. This, in turn, makes us better at leading others.

Now we arrive at the dimension that is at once the most hidden and yet the most crucial to us leading authentically and courageously from our true selves. When I first introduce the spiritual dimension to leaders, they nod their heads in agreement at its importance. And yet as we go on, they find it to be the most difficult dimension to describe and develop. So important, yet so difficult. Indeed, it tends to be the last of the four dimensions about which leaders gain understanding and confidence (figure 8).

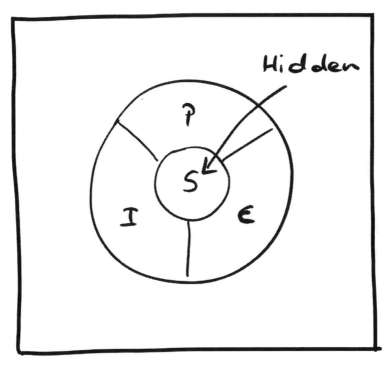

Figure 8. The hidden, but core, spiritual dimension.

WHY THE SPIRITUAL DIMENSION IS THE HARDEST

I see two primary reasons for this difficulty. First, the spiritual dimension is the most intimate and personal of our four dimensions. Only under certain conditions and only with certain people are we willing to open up this part of ourselves to others, much less invite them in to look around and comment on what they see.

I have to be particularly sensitive to this in my work with leaders. Why? Because our coaching partnerships are characterized by complete confidentiality. The safety of such confidentiality enables leaders to explore every aspect of themselves without the concern that they are being judged or assessed.

Even within the safety of this confidentiality, I have to be careful. This is because, whereas all of us are generally open to hearing best practices for our physical fitness, our intellectual thought life, and our emotional health, our spiritual identity and practices remain so personal. If you try to give someone instruction in this area, a common reaction might be "Don't tell me how to be spiritual!"

Second, our spiritual dimension is the most hidden and mysterious of our four dimensions. On the one hand, it is revealing itself all the time through the "surface" dimensions of our physical, intellectual, and emotional selves, greatly influencing how we show up and lead. And yet we have difficulty seeing it, naming it, and ultimately harnessing it to be at our best as leaders.

Crisis reveals character.

Consider what happens in you when your boss criticizes you in front of others, or when everyone in the room ignores your suggestion on how to solve a problem. You feel disrespected, irrelevant, or ignored. And it hits you at your core. The unspoken questions that arise from deep inside you might be "Who do they think I am?" or "Why am I even here?" or "Do they not value me?"

Generally, we recognize our spiritual dimension most easily when we are in circumstances or seasons of intense pressure. During tough times, we jettison niceties and superficial ways of being. Crisis reveals character.

Richard Rohr refers to our "true self" as an "immortal diamond."[20] Diamonds, forged under conditions of tremendous heat and pressure, are the hardest of all natural materials. What gets revealed when your physical, intellectual, and emotional dimensions are under excruciating pressure? Do they cave in? Or does the pressure reveal a strong, sustainable spiritual foundation beneath them?

To take a measure of your spiritual foundation, consider these questions:

- Who am I when my livelihood is threatened?

- Who am I when I witness injustice?

- Who am I when I learn I have a terminal illness?

- Who am I when the building is on fire and everyone is running for the exits?

- Who am I when something goes wrong on my watch?

- Who am I when no one is around to see?

If your life is relatively peaceful right now, it might be hard to answer these questions. The time to do a "stress test" on your identity, values, and character is *not* when everything is peachy and on cruise control. The real test is when the stuff hits the fan, risk is high, and threats are imminent. It's true for you as a leader—and by the way, it is true of the company you lead.

WHAT IS THE SPIRITUAL DIMENSION?

Whole books, secular and sacred, have been written to help you explore and understand your spiritual dimension. In fact, because it is so essential to lead from your core, I hope to write another book devoted to just this topic someday. So while the space of one chapter will limit how far we go, I will try to give you some pathways of entry into this deepest, most essential part of yourself.

However, it is ultimately up to you to continue to blaze trails of your own. Let the questions I pose at the end of each section serve as invitations for you to curiously investigate the "essence" of who you are—your spiritual dimension.

What It Is Not

As a beginning entry point, be careful not to mistake your other three dimensions for your spiritual core. You are not simply your thoughts. You are not simply your emotions. And you are not defined simply by your body. This is critical to understand both the spiritual dimension and the other three dimensions (figure 9).

What happens to the Hollywood actress and the NFL football player when they discover their bodies are no longer considered as valuable by the director or coach as they once were? Do they suddenly lose their identities?

Figure 9. Don't confuse your core spiritual identity with what you do, think, or feel.

In the same way, if you define yourself according to your thoughts and emotions, you will be like a wave tossed on the ocean as changes in circumstances lift and lower your mood. Instead, if you are to be strong and steady on your feet as a leader, you must know who you are with a clarity that withstands changes in your body, your thoughts, and your emotions.

What is it about you that is deeper and more enduring than your physical presence and momentary thoughts and feelings?

The Core of Your "Being"

As mentioned earlier, perhaps the most straightforward way to distinguish the spiritual dimension from the other dimensions is in terms of *being* versus *doing*. The outer three dimensions, the physical, intellectual, and emotional, represent your personality—the external part of yourself that shows up and connects with others (figure 10). These outward dimensions represent all of your "doing."

But awareness of your spiritual dimension takes you from the "doing" of the outer three dimensions into the core of who you are as a human "being." What is there when you sit quietly and do nothing? When you still your body, your thoughts, and your feelings, what do you find?

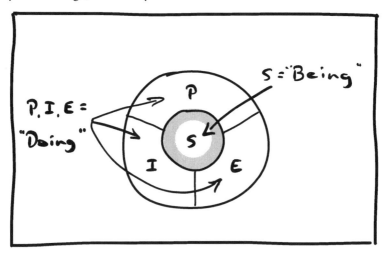

Figure 10. Our spiritual "being" is distinct from the "doing" expressed through our outer three dimensions, the personality dimensions.

This can be a very difficult exercise for many leaders, especially those who define themselves or value their worth by their actions and accomplishments. And yet, in those leaders that connect with their inner core, who find their identities in something deeper than just their accomplishments, we detect a quiet and steady strength that shows through in even the most stressful of circumstances.

> When you still your body, your thoughts, and your feelings, what do you find?

Influenced by Religion but Not Limited by It

Often, when we hear the term "spiritual," we think of religion. Whether you consider yourself Jewish, Catholic, Christian, Buddhist, New Age, or Muslim, if you have a faith, it absolutely colors this dimension.[21]

Religion influences your beliefs about the world and your place in it, it influences your character and your sense of right and wrong, and it gives you rituals and practices to strengthen your spiritual life. But it is not the whole of your spiritual being.

Often, in working with leaders who are devout in their faiths, if I ask, "What are you aware of in your spiritual core right now?" they might tell me how much they have meditated this week or the last time they worshipped in their church or synagogue. Notice these are "doing" activities, not "being."

But I am asking a different question: What are the *contents* of your spiritual dimension—your identity, purpose, values, and beliefs—and how do they affect how you lead? And if you have a faith, how does your faith influence these contents? We'll talk more about each of these aspects later in the chapter.

Authentic Integration

Your spiritual dimension contains who you truly are—your authentic self. Something that is "authentic" is "genuine; real; representing one's true nature or beliefs."[22] So your authentic self is "the real you," independent of how you show up in your other three dimensions to the outside world. We cannot know the truth of who someone is without discerning his or her spiritual core—the human "being" part (figure 11).

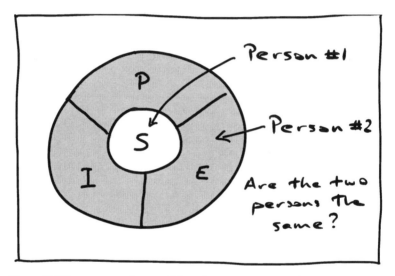

Figure 11. When we are authentic, all four dimensions represent the same person.

If this concept doesn't immediately register for you, I want simply to draw your attention to a long line of well-known individuals who were all esteemed highly at one point and even promoted as role models for the rest of us. These people, "leaders" in one form or another, were doers—performers.

From the corporate heads of such companies as Enron, Tyco, and Theranos, to Bernie Madoff, Bill Cosby, and Lance Armstrong, all of these individuals conveyed one persona outwardly through their physical-intellectual-emotional personality, only to reveal something quite different about what was (or wasn't) in their spiritual cores. They were inauthentic.

Those who follow you are continually scanning to discern who you really are, what you care greatly about, what you believe, and whether it all fits together in an integrated way. The more consistent the evidence they see of your authenticity, the greater chance they will trust you and, in turn, give you their best.

> The more people see you as authentic, the greater chance they will trust you and, in turn, give you their best.

Who are you, really? How does your personality—how you show up in your body, your thoughts, and your feelings—reflect the truth of who you know yourself to be?

Your Spirit

Do you ever regard someone in terms of their "spirit"? "He has such a good spirit about things." "She always brings a great spirit to our meetings." I like Dallas Willard's definition of spirit—"un-embodied personal power."[23] It's often difficult to name precisely what is compelling about a leader's spirit—you just sense it.

Think about the effect of a light bulb. A small, concentrated nucleus of energy lights up a whole room, touching every surface exposed to it. It is difficult to contain light completely. It affects everything to which it is exposed. When people say, "There is something different about him," they are speaking of what emanates from a person's spiritual core, through the person's personality and out into the world.

Connected to Something Bigger

I once sat in the audience with my daughter listening to the late John McCain take questions at a Veterans Day event at a local university.[24] A young boy went to the microphone and asked the senator, "I am pursuing my Eagle Scout badge; do you have any advice for me?" McCain replied, "My advice for you would simply be this. If you want to have an impact in life, you have to be living for something bigger than yourself." This from a man who was a prisoner of war for five and a half years.

> What is it "about you" that touches others? What do others experience when they are in your presence?

I suggest, unless you consider yourself to be the center of your universe, that your spiritual dimension is where you connect with "something or someone bigger than yourself." To live otherwise is like inserting the plug end of a power strip back into the power strip!

Who or what guides you? What is your enduring source of inspiration and power?

I hope the section above helped you tap into your experience of the spiritual dimension. Now I'd like to encourage you to understand yourself better by clarifying four key aspects of your spiritual dimension: your identity, your purpose, your beliefs, and your values.

SPIRITUAL SELF-LEADERSHIP CHALLENGE I: KNOW WHO YOU ARE—IDENTITY

📝 "JOURNAL TIME"

Go to LeadLikeYouBook.com for an exercise related to this challenge.

"Who am I?"

Wow, what a big question! It seems so simple and yet so complex and overwhelming at the same time. A good number of leaders I work with have no clue how to answer this question—including those with "CEO" and "president" after their names. They are very good at answering "What do I do?" but get stumped with "Who am I?" In fact, they will often turn it around to me and say, "Who do you think I am?"

Once, within a few days of one another, I had conversations with two different men, each accomplished leaders. They each recalled vividly the voices of their fathers, who were both deceased.

One leader, in his late fifties, recalled his father saying to him, "You can do anything you want, but you won't. You are all talk."

The other, in his late thirties, had heard, "Son, you are the best."

You might think one father's words were a curse, the other a blessing. Interestingly, the younger leader spoke of how his father's words—"You are the best"—had actually driven him to think he *had* to be the best at everything he did. What was intended as a blessing had become a burden.

Whenever someone says to us, "You are . . . ," they are likely speaking into the domain of our spiritual being, speaking of our essence. If it is a positive word, we are inspired and blessed. If negative, we are hurt, often deeply.

As a side note, I believe that we are all wired to receive "a blessing" that speaks into our being from the two people who brought us into this world, our parents—especially our fathers. Many of us received a word of some kind from our fathers: affirming, belittling, or somewhere in between. Others of us never received a word because our fathers were not there, which had its own effect as well.

Pause for a moment to consider your story. What words did you hear, or did you not hear, from your parents? How has that impacted who you have become as a leader?

Who do others say that you are? How does this show up in your daily leadership?

Who are you?

Regardless of the words of your parents, or other influences upon your spiritual identity, I offer you two pathways to begin to answer this question of "Who am I?" for yourself. The first is to think of your identity in terms of your "voice." What is your voice in the room? At the conference table? When you speak, what comes out—besides just the words?

Parker J. Palmer has written a whole book on this notion of voice, called, appropriately, *Let Your Life Speak: Listening for the Voice of Vocation.* One of my favorite takeaways is where he talks about the Latin root for the word "voice"—*voce.* It is from this root that our word "vocation" comes.[25]

We all want to "get busy" with our careers, to "build" our resumes, and to "create" our vocation. But Palmer suggests that vocation, something we devote our lives to and from which we derive much of our identity, begins with listening for a voice that arises. He says, be quiet and listen! Listen for your own voice that wants to speak and change the world around you.

A second way to home in on your identity is to think in terms of the different roles you play in life. Consider Dan. Dan may be president of a large division, but he could also be a husband, father, son, brother, best friend, volunteer, and neighbor.

As a son, he may manage the finances of an elderly parent. As a husband, he may listen to his wife as she considers what she wants to do after the kids leave home for college. As a president, he may challenge his people to accomplish things they never thought possible and then make sure they are praised when they do. As a neighbor, he may see to it that the elderly widow down the street never has to shovel her own walk after a snowfall.

One person, many roles. But there is probably some consistency with which this one person expresses himself in his various roles. These common traits intersect in identity (figure 12).

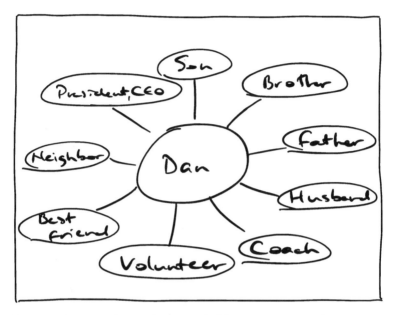

Figure 12. One way to discern identity is to look for common traits in the various roles you fill in life.

What roles do you fill in life? What is your identity in each of those roles? What is consistent about your identity across all the roles?

If you can begin to find similarities in who you are to the people you serve in each of your roles, you are probably closing in on your essence, your identity.

Many years ago, Marta and I were taking a morning walk. At the time, I was struggling in my career, and frankly, I was struggling with my identity. (Up to that time, I had defined myself largely by my career—hence the twin struggles!) I shared my concerns with her that sunny spring morning.

Suddenly, Marta asked me a direct question: "Who are you when you coach your clients?" Without a whole lot of hesitation, I blurted out, "Well . . . , I'm a confidante . . . , an advisor . . . , and an encourager!"

Over the coming days, I realized that those words were spoken by the true voice of my spiritual dimension. I have sat with those three words now for over a decade, and they still ring true for me today—transcending my vocation as a coach, and capturing who I am as husband, father, son, friend, seatmate, dinner guest, and more!

What are some of the first thoughts that come to mind as you think about your identity that begin to answer the question "Who am I?" You don't need to have the "perfect" answer or something that makes sense to others. Simply respond with what is meaningful and true to *you*.

SPIRITUAL SELF-LEADERSHIP CHALLENGE 2: KNOW WHY YOU ARE HERE—PURPOSE

> "JOURNAL TIME"
>
> Go to LeadLikeYouBook.com for an exercise related to this challenge.

Think about a meeting you participated in this week—not as just an audience member but as an active participant, whether as a leader or a follower. Why were *you* in that meeting? What did you contribute to the meeting, whether it was a large or small contribution?

I ask this question of CEOs often to help them be sure they are staying focused. I ask, "What does your company need that only you can provide?"

Earlier, I wrote about your "voice" in the room and what it says about who you are—your identity. Here we turn to the "why" of your spiritual core. Why is it important that you are here, that your voice be heard? What is your purpose? In a questionnaire I give to all my leaders before I coach them, I ask, "Why does your business exist?"

In this context, I ask you, why do *you* exist? There is a reason, it's a good one, and it's important you figure it out. As with everything else in the spiritual dimension, this is not something that is just "nice to know." It's critical to know, because it directly affects your leadership effectiveness.

Why do you exist?

Purpose provides meaning and motivation. We talked earlier about living your life for something or someone bigger than yourself. I can wake up in the morning and think just about myself—*my* to-do list, *my* schedule, *my* worries, or *my* golf game—which candidly does not bring me sustainable inspiration! But when I calibrate with my purpose, and how my actions and words might help others, that gives meaning to my day and fires me up!

Purpose simplifies things. Leaders who are disconnected from their purpose feel they have to be all things to all people, and they spend their time running around trying to fulfill everyone else's expectations. But those who lead on purpose tend to show up where and when they are most needed. And they spend more time resting in between!

Purpose helps us get through tough times. Often, when things get tough, they are tough on us personally. The more difficult they are, the more we can feel like we are slipping into a deep hole, helpless and maybe forgotten by others. This inward focus tends to amplify how negatively we see things. According to researchers, having a purpose in life is a key contributor to resilience and helps us avoid succumbing to difficult circumstances.[26]

Purpose leads to high impact. Clarity of purpose results in me staying in my "purpose-driven zone" more often. I stay alert for opportunities to live and lead on purpose. This requires turning off the autopilot and tuning in to people and situations where, drawing from my spiritual core, I can have the greatest impact. Whatever we focus on tends to grow.

Like everything else in the spiritual dimension, purpose is unique to each one of us. There's no one formula for instantly discovering your purpose. But don't let that deter you from returning regularly to work on the question "What is my purpose—why do I exist?"

As with identity, I encourage leaders to allow their purpose to "marinate." Start by adding a few ingredients, and then allow the passage of time, some stirring, and the application of a little "heat" (stress or difficulty) to yield a flavorful result.

Here are some statements to help you identify the beginning ingredients:

- I feel most alive when . . .
- I want to be remembered for . . . but I especially want to be remembered for . . .
- I am totally in my zone when . . .
- I feel most fulfilled when . . .
- I find my greatest joy in . . .
- If money were no object, I would like to spend more/all of my time doing . . .
- I want my legacy to be . . .
- If I knew I had only three months to live, I would make sure I . . .

Write down the words and phrases that come to mind. Don't overanalyze them, and don't be concerned about what anyone else will think. Your true purpose is like buried treasure inside you. Keep digging to find it!

SPIRITUAL SELF-LEADERSHIP CHALLENGE 3: EXAMINE YOUR BELIEFS

> 📝 **"JOURNAL TIME"**
>
> *Go to LeadLikeYouBook.com for an exercise related to this challenge.*

I will never forget the first time Marta and I got into a heated argument. It began as we were going through the cafeteria line one day in college, and it carried over to the table when we sat down. We were fiercely debating a hot political topic at the time, and our voices rose as we went back and forth on opposite sides of the issue.

At one point I finally said, "How can you believe that?!" We were so opposed in our beliefs that I wondered if we could continue dating if we saw things so differently. Up to that point, I had thought we were so compatible!

Needless to say, we moved past that issue, continued dating, married, and have been together ever since. Here's the interesting observation I have made years later. Marta was able to articulate why she believed what she believed, whereas my belief was one that I had never questioned or examined. I had "inherited" my belief from my father. I enthusiastically defended something I had never really paused to examine or consider why it was mine.

Each of us navigates life with a broad portfolio of beliefs that serve as the foundation and filter for how we *perceive* (see); how we *process* what we perceive; and finally, how we *present* ourselves (show up) as a result. Beliefs are the underpinning for how we think, feel, and act in the intellectual, emotional, and physical dimensions. Yet how often do we pause, reflect, and examine our beliefs to be sure we are living and leading consistently with them?

Before I begin work with leaders, I send them a fairly exhaustive questionnaire that prepares them for coaching and tells me a little about them. One of the questions on page 7 is "What are three to five foundational or universal principles you currently use as a structure for how you lead?"

I ask this softball question to help leaders begin to examine their beliefs. Here are how some recent leaders have answered the question:

- Lead by example.
- Be moral.
- Be fair.
- Be humble.
- Be kind.
- If you're nice to other people, they'll be nice to you.
- Let people know you appreciate them.
- Be clear about what you expect from your employees/kids.
- Be willing to get your hands dirty.
- Be as honest with yourself and others as possible.
- Be as communicative and open as possible.
- People's time is their most vital commodity, so you shouldn't waste it.
- Don't fight for the last nickel in a deal.
- Be sincere.
- Do the right thing.
- Value relationships.
- Respect others.

- Be open-minded.
- Be a great family member.
- Be a good/strong/successful worker.
- Be a good citizen.
- Be healthy.

How recently have you paused to reflect on the foundational beliefs that influence how you lead? For most, my guess is it has been a while. And yet isn't this like the whole of the spiritual dimension? It can be mysterious and elusive to pin down, yet it is absolutely influencing our every move, every day!

The realm of what you believe is vast. Religions are devoted to it. Societies are held together by it. So for our purposes here, I will set some helpful boundaries to encourage you to explore without being overwhelmed. Here are three pathways for you to more deeply explore or notice your beliefs.

What Guides You?

When you sit at the conference table with your team and say that "we have to do it this way" or "we must avoid that," what is behind the "have to" and the "must"? Generally, there are beliefs behind these strong words and the emotions that frequently accompany them.

Consider a discussion about a new sales campaign between two leaders who hold these opposing views:

- One believes that "everyone deserves a chance."

- The other believes that "only those who work hard deserve a chance."

How might these underlying, and unspoken, beliefs influence how each of the leaders thinks, feels, speaks, and behaves as they construct the sales campaign?

Begin to get better at noticing what guides you. As you champion a new project or defend against a change in strategy, what beliefs underlie your arguments?

What Would You Sacrifice For?

Taking it a step further, what beliefs are so core that they would cause you to sacrifice in some way? Perhaps an ethical belief would cause you to be the only one in a group who speaks up and says "No!" Or a belief about what is just and fair would prompt you to intervene. How about a belief in what it means to be a good dad that has you risking embarrassment as you leave the office before others do?

If challenged, what beliefs would you stand up for?

The sacrifice test can identify the types of beliefs we hold and measure how deeply they penetrate. These beliefs keep us grounded when everyone else is wishy-washy. People want to follow leaders who are grounded, principled, and dependable. (This happens to be one of my beliefs—you can agree or not!) If challenged, what beliefs would you stand up for?

What Do You Need to Remind Yourself Of?

We are all prone to forget. The tyranny of the urgent crowds out the important—even the remembrance of the important.

Leaders who act with integrity, whose outer actions and words are consistent with their inner beliefs, have habits for reminding themselves on a regular basis what they believe. One of the roles of churches, synagogues, and other places of worship is to serve as gathering places for remembering and discussing beliefs and how to put them into action. Some leaders read books or include quiet moments of meditation in their daily schedules. Others have lunch once a month with a friend who helps them stay grounded.

What do you do on a regular basis to remember your core beliefs? Are your life and leadership aligned with these beliefs?

SPIRITUAL SELF-LEADERSHIP CHALLENGE 4: KNOW WHAT YOU REALLY WANT—VALUES

"JOURNAL TIME"

Go to LeadLikeYouBook.com for an exercise related to this challenge.

I am thinking of my work with Clay, the young COO of a large, closely held company. As he was transitioning into his COO role, he was still building his relationship with the longtime CEO, Peter.

More than once, I have heard Clay say to me that he wants the flexibility and control over his calendar to leave work and be with his family at critical times. Such flexibility would result in him not working late some days and on others leaving during normal business hours to attend one of his children's plays or soccer games.

On the other side, CEO Peter, who tends to work long hours, has complained several times to me that Clay sometimes gets up and walks out of meetings or leaves the office early with no explanation.

There's something going on here that will either continue to frustrate each of them or, through healthy dialogue, get resolved. What is it? Is Clay just lazy? Is he pressured by a wife who complains he should have a better work-life balance? Or is Peter such a workaholic that he simply expects everyone else to put in the same long hours he does?

Actually, Clay is very driven. Like many leaders I know, he places a high value on working hard to accomplish a lot and be successful. But he values something even more: his family. As much as you or I would also say we value family, Clay's value of family is possibly even more profound.

Clay's parents divorced when he was young. His mom ran away with another man, and Clay grew up with his dad, who eventually married a woman who was the worst kind of step-mother a young boy could have. Clay never knew a loving, supportive family environment growing up.

Eventually, he met and married a wonderful woman, Susan, and they had three kids together. Clay has been very committed to loving his wife and bringing up those three kids in the loving home he never knew.

Then guess what happened? Two years ago, Clay was home with the kids while Susan was away on a business trip. He was awakened in the middle of the night with a startling phone call. Susan had been in a bad car accident and was in the ICU of a hospital in another city.

He almost lost Susan. It took her nearly a year to fully recover from her injuries. Only recently have their lives started to become normal again.

Clay had worked very hard for something he never had—family. And then suddenly he was faced with losing it all again. The value he places on family is extraordinary. He will do whatever he needs to do to preserve and grow it. This is why he wants the flexibility to leave work at times and be with his family. Eventually, he will need to have a conversation with Peter to address the at times conflicting values of family and work.

Are you clear about the values you treasure most? Can you articulate the top three things you value above everything else? The top one?

If not, go to LeadLikeYouBook.com to take our values exercise.

You probably value many things, but what values rise to the very top? What would you fight for or defend? These are the trump cards of your life. When you're really under pressure, you will play them. Since they have so much influence on you, wouldn't it be a good idea to have clarity on what they are?

What do you value most?

THE SPIRITUAL DIMENSION OF COMPANIES

I cannot close out this chapter without pointing out that what is true for you as a leader in the spiritual dimension is also true for companies. Great companies know their identities, their purpose, their beliefs and guiding principles, and their values. They simply change the language slightly (table 4).

Individual	Corporate	Answers
Identity	Brand	Who?
Purpose	Mission	Why?
Beliefs/Values	Culture	How?

Table 4. The elements of our spiritual dimension parallel the elements of Brand, Mission and Culture in an organization.

Just as company teams "go away" to reflect and discuss this "soft stuff" that is so important, you as a four-dimensional leader must also create time to pause and reflect on what is guiding you, ideally on a daily basis.

Now that we have examined this deepest dimension in ourselves, as well as the outer three dimensions that surround it, let's look at how to put them all together so we can lead with our best selves on any given day.

KEY TAKEAWAYS

- My spiritual dimension is the most hidden and mysterious of my four dimensions. And yet it has the greatest influence on whether I lead authentically and courageously from my true self.

- Difficult circumstances are likely to expose what is in my spiritual dimension.

- The core of my being, who I truly am, resides in my spiritual dimension. When I am authentic, my spiritual dimension aligns with—that is, is consistent with—my other three dimensions.

- There are four key components of my spiritual dimension:

    - my identity, which answers the question "Who am I?"

    - my purpose, which answers the question "Why am I here?"

    - my beliefs, which answer the question "What do I believe?"

- my values, which answer the question "What do I really want?"

- Gaining clarity on the components of my spiritual dimension takes time.

QUESTIONS FOR REFLECTION

- Recall a very difficult season in your life, or a stressful event that happened more recently. What did the challenge reveal about who you really are at your (spiritual) core?

- How well would you say the people around you know who you really are? Why?

- For what do you want to be known?

- What practices do you have at present that help you focus on your identity, purpose, values, and beliefs?

- How might more intentional work in this area help you be a more effective leader?

- Go back to your Recent Regrettable Leadership Experience in chapter 2. What do you notice now about how you were showing up—spiritually?

- **Go to LeadLikeYouBook.com for additional exercises related to this chapter.**

CHAPTER 7

FOUR-DIMENSIONAL AWARENESS: PUTTING IT ALL TOGETHER

Know thyself.
—Inscription on the Greek Temple
of Apollo at Delphi

*The soul speaks its truth only under quiet,
inviting, and trustworthy conditions.*
—Parker J. Palmer, *Let Your Life Speak*

I had begun coaching a new CEO, and five weeks into our engagement, much of our time had been spent helping her grow her self-awareness in the four dimensions you have been reading about.

Later, on the day of one of our coaching sessions, she was to lead a board meeting. Interestingly, we did not spend any time helping her prepare for that board meeting. Instead, we drilled more on self-awareness.

The next day, unprompted by me, she sent this text: "I was told today that the board meeting I presided over was my best yet and that I had command of the room! Thought you'd like to hear that. I am pleased. It's starting to work!"

I smiled.

I have been teaching four-dimensional self-awareness to leaders for years. And I suspect that, if you are like many of them, you are now ready to do something with what you have been reading. After all, as a leader, that is how you are wired, right? To get things done? To accomplish? Let's go, already!

Well, becoming more aware, especially in all four dimensions, tends to slow things down a bit. And that is intentional. If you want to grow and change as a leader, you must do things differently. To do things differently requires intentional choice. You can only choose intentionally if you pause the autopilot, notice where you are, and realize that you have options for how you act or react. Remember that, at any given time, you are either on autopilot or you are aware.

So you want to do something? The very first thing you can do is become a master at being aware. Become an expert at noticing. Mastering awareness is the first step toward becoming an effective four-dimensional leader. If you will slow down and do this, then, like so many other leaders I have coached over the years, you will begin to change and lead differently, within one week—guaranteed.

I can say this because I receive eyewitness reports every week from the leaders I work with, like the young CEO above or the people they lead:

- From the leader: "I noticed I was getting angry with the same person I always get angry with, but I paused and chose to respond without raising my voice."

- From the leader's direct report: "I don't know what you're doing with Todd, but we've already noticed a difference in him, for the better!"

Here's the secret. All I did was help these leaders be more aware. Then the leaders, being smart, chose to act in a way that was more resourceful—for themselves and for the people they influence.

At the end of each of the previous four chapters, I gave you questions for reflection to help you become more aware in each of the four dimensions. Those were an introduction to awareness of each of the four dimensions. Your task now, at this point in the book, is to begin to become a master of being aware. Think about it. If you were strong in every aspect of your job except in understanding and using financial statements, you would figure out a way to get smarter about financial statements. Or if your boss told you that you need to become more strategic, more visionary, you would figure out how to get better at strategy.

You may have heard that it takes ten thousand hours to achieve mastery level at something.[27] Simply understanding the concept of being aware doesn't mean you've mastered it. To master awareness, and thus move on to master each of the four dimensions, you must practice and practice until it becomes second nature. Pause now briefly and tune in to your body, your thoughts, your feelings, and your spirit. The more you do this—turning off autopilot and becoming aware—the more naturally you can incorporate it into your leadership and become a better leader.

SECOND-NATURE AWARENESS

Can you think of something you tried that was difficult at first, but eventually, with practice, it became second nature? I think of different times over the years I've tried a new workout gym or program. The first time you go into the room, it takes time to figure out all kinds of things: the right weight to use, how many repetitions, how to adjust the seat, and in what sequence to do the exercises.

But then, after two to three weeks of consecutive use, and recording what you do each time, you walk in and move effortlessly from one station to another—knowing exactly how much weight to use, how to adjust the machine, and how many reps per set. The whole workout probably takes less time, and you do everything with more self-confidence.

Practicing awareness may feel a little awkward and clunky at first, but with repetition it will become more and more automatic. Every time you practice awareness, you pause the autopilot and consciously consider your next step, which leads to new possibilities.

Anytime Is a Good Time for Being Aware

The great thing about becoming a master at four-dimensional awareness is that you can practice anytime, anywhere, and no one else has to know you're practicing! Whether you're lying in bed, walking down the hall to the conference room, sitting quietly on your back porch on a springtime Saturday morning, or heading toward the baggage claim at LaGuardia, anytime is a good time to practice being aware.

> You can practice four-dimensional awareness anytime, anywhere.

In fact, *now* is a good time to practice. See the questions below to help you check in with yourself. Take at least five minutes to consider these prompts. (Later, after we cover the additional steps of assessing and adjusting, I recommend you visit LeadLikeYouBook.com for an electronic version of these questions, as well as additional resources to help you be aware, assess, and then adjust to be at your leadership best.) Pause and notice the dimensions.

Physical. Use the questions to notice what is going on in your body:

- How am I doing physically (i.e., hungry, thirsty, tired, sick, sore, rested, healthy or energetic)?
- How is my posture?
- What is my position in the room relative to others?
- What is the look on my face?
- What am I doing with my hands (or other body parts)?
- Am I leaning toward or away from others?
- Am I tense? Where?
- How is my breathing?
- When others look at me, what do they see?
- On a scale of one to ten (where ten is high), what is my stress level?

Intellectual. Use these questions to notice what is going on in your head:

- What is foremost on my mind? Is it good? Is it true?
- What else am I thinking about in the background (perhaps something in the recent past or near future)?
- What am I thinking about my current activity?
- What am I thinking about other people?

- What am I thinking about myself?
- How am I processing my thoughts (e.g., creatively, randomly, or logically)?
- What are my most powerful thoughts?

Emotional. Use these questions to notice what is going on in your heart:

- What emotion am I feeling right now (i.e., glad, sad, mad, scared, or ashamed)?
- Am I feeling or ignoring my emotions?
- Is there a situation or a person not in my presence that is also affecting my emotions?
- Am I letting my emotions show?
- Am I passionate about what I am currently doing or the topic being discussed?
- What emotion might others detect in me? How might they detect it?

Spiritual. Use these questions to notice what is going on in your core:

- Who am I? How is my identity connected with my current activity?
- Why do I exist? How consistent is my current activity with my overall sense of purpose?
- What do I believe? What role do my beliefs play in my current activity?
- What do I value? How are my values reflected in my current activity?
- Do I manifest on the outside (physically, intellectually, and emotionally) what is true on the inside (spiritually)?

Here are other opportunities to pause and build awareness into the fabric of your day:

- sitting early in the morning before others are awake, perhaps in a special room or chair
- driving to work in the morning instead of talking on your phone
- preparing just before and debriefing after a big conversation, meeting, or presentation
- driving home from work, reflecting on your day, learning from it, and transitioning toward evening activities
- lying in your bed, waiting to fall asleep

Extreme Situations Are the Best Times for Awareness

When I get on the phone with leaders for a coaching session, especially early in our relationships, I ask them to reflect back on the past week and identify a situation when they were at their best or their worst. Although anytime can be a good time for awareness, extreme situations are the best. Extremes help us see things more clearly (figure 13).

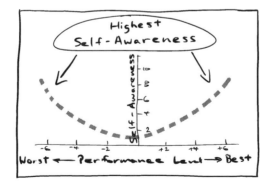

Figure 13. Self-awareness is usually highest at times when our performance is extremely good or extremely bad.

And so it is when practicing four-dimensional awareness. If you take time to tune in to those days or events when you are completely in your groove as a leader—when you are strong, effective, and confident—you have the opportunity to notice the conditions in yourself that helped make that happen. And guess what? You, being the smart leader you are, will work to repeat those conditions more often so that you spend more of your days at your best.

By the same token, when you use four-dimensional awareness to review a day in the life of your leadership that you would rather do over—or completely forget!—you grow your ability to avoid those contributing conditions in yourself in the future.

Extreme situations shine the light more brightly on the same dynamics occurring in between the extremes. In a "me-at-my-worst" scenario, intense anger and losing my temper may have been the emotional contributor. But likely, I'm also carrying a low level of anger—call it "frustration"—on a daily basis. I just don't notice it as much as I do in the more extreme situations.

Let's consider Maria, a leader who used four-dimensional awareness to prepare for an off-site strategy session with her team. The day was a tremendous success. Afterward, she reviews the "extremely good" day and her part in it, using the four dimensions.

Maria recalls that she entered the day intentionally aware that "I am a consensus builder," her identity in the spiritual dimension. With reflection, she realizes that, though it took a while for the team to coalesce around a strategy, in the end, her intentionality as a consensus builder was key to her team reaching agreement. Her ability to build consensus, indeed, is an important part of who she is.

Having realized this ability in an extreme situation, Maria will probably notice more, on a day-to-day basis, that she routinely helps build consensus among people with different points of view. Now she can be more intentional about applying this strength all the time, not just at big events like strategy off-sites. Her everyday effectiveness as a leader grows.

WHY THE FOUR-DIMENSIONAL DIAGRAM MATTERS

Recently, I introduced the four-dimensional leadership model to Susan, a company president and new client. I shared with her much of what I have shared with you up to this point: Real growth requires change. Change requires turning off the autopilot and choosing to show up and behave differently. Consciously choosing requires awareness. Self-awareness comes more easily when we break things down and begin to pay attention to and lead ourselves using the four dimensions.

I could tell Susan was tracking with me. As I completed my overview of the four dimensions and drew the circular diagram (figure 14), she asked, "Why do you illustrate it that way? Why not simply four boxes or something else?"

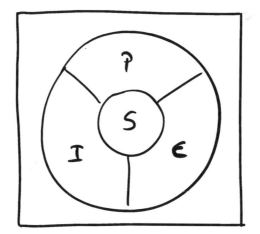

Figure 14. Diagram of the four dimensions.

I loved her question. Susan was engaged. She was also thoughtful and curious. And if she was going to buy into this model, really own it, she wanted to understand why it was portrayed as a circle and not some other geometric shape. Indeed, the reason I illustrate the four dimensions the way I do is quite intentional.

I've already mentioned that I diagram the four dimensions in this way because I believe the spiritual dimension represents the core of ourselves expressed through the other three dimensions. Here I'd like to explain this diagram in more detail. But before I do, let me pause and acknowledge that the notion that we have four aspects of ourselves—a body, a brain, a heart, and a soul—is nothing new. In fact, it is ancient.

When I share the four-dimensional leadership model with my observant Jewish friends, many of them instantly think of the Shema, the most important prayer in Judaism—"Hear O Israel: the Lord our God, the Lord is one. You shall love the Lord your God with all your heart, with all your soul, and with all your strength. . . ."[28]

And when I am with my Christian friends, I remind them of both the Old Testament passage where the Shema appears and its New Testament companion, "Love the Lord your God with all your heart . . . soul . . . mind . . . and strength."[29] These two admonitions from these ancient faiths are at least 3,400 and 1,900 years old, respectively.

Others who teach on these dimensions diagram the relationship between the four differently. Unlike Susan, you may have no curiosity about why I illustrate the four dimensions as I do, but I actually find the comparison between my four dimensions diagram and others' versions to be useful as a way to better understand how all four dimensions come together and interact.

The most basic diagram we typically see used to illustrate the four dimensions is a matrix with four quadrants (figure

15). In this diagram, each dimension is equal and undifferenti-
ated in relationship to the other three.

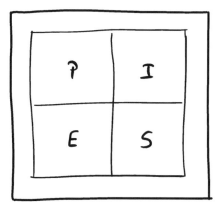

Figure 15. The four dimensions diagrammed as a four-quadrant matrix.

Another diagram sometimes used illustrates the four
dimensions as interlocking circles (figure 16). This image suggests overlap and influence between the four dimensions, as
well as a "self" that is separate from the spiritual dimension
in the center where all four intersect. Like the matrix illustration above, there is no hierarchy of the dimensions or a greater
influence of one dimension over the other three.

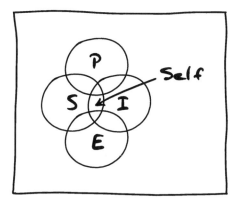

Figure 16. The four dimensions diagrammed as interlocking circles.

Last, I have seen the dimensions illustrated in the form of a pyramid, with physical being at the foundation level, then building with emotional, intellectual, and spiritual at the very top (figure 17). Aspects of this model resonate with me: at a foundational level, how we are doing physically has a powerful impact on how we are doing in the other dimensions, and at the highest level, the spiritual dimension can be the toughest to access and understand. But the diagram suggests either a top-down or bottom-up stair-step relationship between the four.

Figure 17. The four dimensions diagrammed as a pyramid.

So there are a variety of good ways to illustrate the four dimensions. Let me share with you why I have chosen to illustrate them as I do (figure 18).

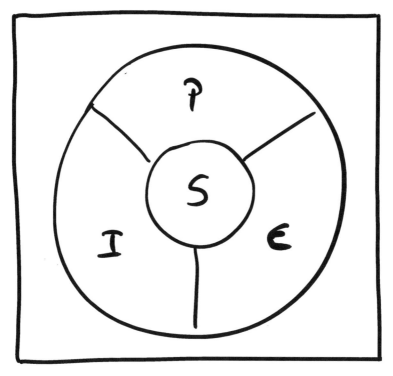

Figure 18. The author's preferred diagram of the four dimensions.

The inner spiritual dimension is concealed behind the other three but drives everything. Based on my observations, one thing we all have in common is that we are constantly self-protecting and self-promoting. Some of us are quite obvious about it. Others of us camouflage it better. But we all have different methods of protecting and promoting ourselves, and these different ways serve as the basis for many of our individually held beliefs. Some leaders "believe" you survive best through serving and pleasing others. Some by intimidating or dominating. Some by outsmarting others.

This "self" we try to protect or promote is our identity in the inner spiritual dimension, and it tells the "outer" dimensions, "Protect me! Keep me safe!" or "Be sure people know I'm here!" Our spiritual dimension, whatever its contents, belongs at the center of the four dimensions.

The outer three dimensions (physical, intellectual, and emotional) represent our personality. In contrast to the spiritual, which is concealed, the other three dimensions are "exposed." People experience us through these three outer dimensions—a combination of our physical presence, our intellectual thoughts expressed as words, and our feelings conveyed through both our body and our language. Taken together, these make up our personality (figure 19).

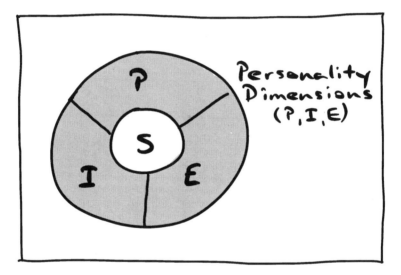

Figure 19. Our personality is represented in our outer three dimensions: physical, intellectual, and emotional.

Through our "personality dimensions," we interact most directly with the world around us—with bosses, customers, direct reports, friends, and family. And daily, we experience pressure from the world around us to be beautiful, handsome, or strong (physical); to be smart (intellectual); and to be happy and emotionally balanced (emotional). When the world presses in, do you cave, or do you press back? How do you respond to these pressures and to these voices (figure 20)?

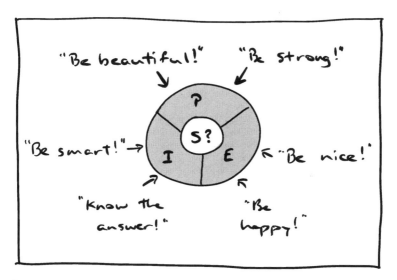

Figure 20. Our outer three dimensions interact directly with the outside world.

Almost weekly we hear sensational stories of the former Hollywood actress who is drug-addicted and penniless. The pro athlete arrested for domestic abuse or homicide. The high-profile CEO fired for falsifying his resume. The Wall Street financier committing suicide.

Yet all around us are less extreme versions of these stories, lived by those listening to outside voices more than their own voices.

Your own voice, your identity, is found in your spiritual dimension. If it is robust and well developed, it serves as the unseen backbone or foundation supporting your outer dimensions (figure 21). Strong leaders work daily to build a substantive spiritual dimension that reinforces their outer personality dimensions. These leaders stand tall in the midst of crisis rather than cave in; "do the right thing," even when it is unpopular or risky; and are at peace with themselves regardless of the storms around them.

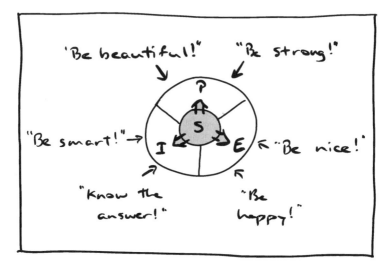

Figure 21. A strong spiritual core tells the outer three dimensions how to respond to the demands the world makes of us.

A great leader needs strength in all four dimensions. I hope this is apparent to you by now. And yet, as I will describe in the next chapter, most senior leaders I have worked with have a "default dimension" that tends to be their favorite—and this default dimension will be one of the three outer personality dimensions.

But to favor one dimension and ignore the others is like driving with a flat tire—you will get to your destination, but you won't arrive in the best of shape, and you won't be prepared for what comes next.

Think about this example: as a leader helping your team navigate change, you can possess self-confidence (spiritual) and have a great plan (intellectual), but if you are angry (emotional) and bullying in your behavior (physical) as you force the plan on others, you will fail to win your team's full engagement.

Another example: you can feel passionately (emotional) about the need to change strategy in order to turn around sales. But if you view your identity as more of a marketeer than a strategist (spiritual), and you fail to develop a well-thought-out plan (intellectual), you will lack credibility with your team, regardless of how good looking or charming a presenter (physical) you might be.

Credibility, authenticity, power, integrity, and presence: such leadership attributes require that all four dimensions are present and at work in a leader from the inside out.

The four dimensions influence one another. In our illustration of the four dimensions, each of the dimensions touches the other three, showing how much each influences the others (figure 22). Which comes first, thinking bad thoughts about myself (intellectual), or feeling badly (emotional)? Not thinking of myself as a runner (intellectual and spiritual), or not running (physical)? They are all intertwined. In chapter 10, we will talk about strategically using the fact that the dimensions impact one another when we consider how to "adjust" toward being in a better place to lead.

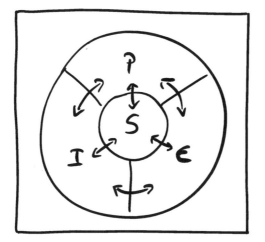

Figure 22. Each dimension influences and is influenced by the other three.

A Side Note on the Physical Dimension

While all the dimensions are necessary, and all influence one another, perhaps the dimension that most easily jump-starts the other three and is a leading indicator of breakdown is the physical dimension.

For example, the physical action of changing into athletic clothing and heading out for a run inevitably leads our other three dimensions to a better place. We start running, the "feel good" endorphins kick in, we feel better about ourselves, our minds open up, and we can get downright heroic in our anticipation of conquering the world!

The flip side also occurs with high frequency. Often, when we get off our game intellectually or emotionally, it is preceded by not taking care of ourselves physically. We skip workouts, attempt to cheat on sleep, eat the wrong kinds of foods, and drink too much of the wrong kinds of liquids—and the next thing we know, we're feeling frustrated or anxious, struggling to stay sharp in our thinking and problem solving.

The Path from Beliefs to Results

Alexander Caillet, a member of the faculty I studied under at Georgetown University, provides a great model of the linkage between our three outer dimensions—intellectual, emotional, and physical—and our results.[30] I alter his model slightly by adding the role of the fourth dimension—spiritual, as in figure 23. Our beliefs and values influence how we think about things.

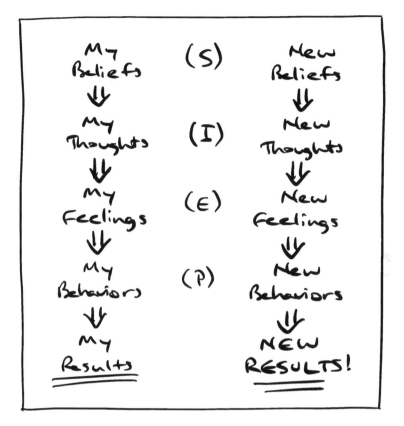

Figure 23. One model for how the four dimensions operate together to produce results.

Caillet's contention: if you want different results, what different behaviors do you need, what feelings do those require, what thoughts are needed to generate those feelings, and finally (my addition), how do your beliefs need to shift to create those thoughts? This model provides a helpful way to see how our beliefs, or our spiritual dimension, truly drives everything.

The Goal: Strength and Balance

If you followed my suggestion to watch the movie *Gladiator* and observe the four dimensions in action, you saw the opening scene where the soldiers sound off to one another, "Strength and honor!" Well, our rallying cry around the four dimensions is "strength and balance!"

First, we want to evaluate the question "How strong am I in each dimension?" We'll talk more about this evaluation in chapter 9, where we discuss assessment. For now, I think you would agree that you are at your best if you are operating at full *strength* physically, intellectually, emotionally, and spiritually.

Second, *balance* across the four dimensions is essential. It is not enough to be really strong in two or three dimensions and flat in the rest. Elite athletes do not get to the top of their game on brute physical strength alone. No, they also happen to be really smart (intellectual), they know how to channel their feelings (emotional), and they believe in themselves (spiritual).

When I wrote this, it was springtime, and top golfers were gathered in Augusta, Georgia, to compete in the Masters. These players are the best golfers in the world. Yet the tangible challenge of the fairways, obstacles, and greens tests so much more than just their physical ability to hit the ball well. Intellectually, they must be sharp on distance as they navigate from tee box to green and then through the undulations of the greens as they aim for the hole. Emotionally, they self-manage to avoid getting too high or too low following great shots and not-so-great shots. And spiritually, they have to believe in themselves and specifically believe they can win. Ultimately, the player at the top of the leaderboard when the play ends on Sunday will have been strong and balanced in each of the four dimensions—they will have mastered themselves and brought their full game.

IMMEDIATE BENEFITS OF MASTERING AWARENESS

If you are like most leaders I introduce to the process of four-dimensional awareness, you have probably already identified some low-hanging fruit. Here are some examples of comments I hear in the early "self-awareness" weeks of coaching a leader:

- "I never realized how my face is so stern all the time, as if I'm angry . . . when I'm not!"

- "I'm aware that I feel a low level of anxiety at all times, and that influences how I show up."

- "I notice I'm always thinking about how to accomplish more in a day. Frankly, it feels overwhelming."

- "I had never connected my sense that 'I don't belong' or 'I don't deserve to be here' with how I view my identity."

If any of these comments ring true for you, I encourage you to stay in the awareness mode and not rush to assessing or adjusting quite yet, because I suspect there could be even more to notice—more layers of the proverbial onion to be peeled back. And the deeper our awareness penetrates, the greater the impact when we make adjustments!

Remember, becoming an expert at awareness is the necessary first step to becoming a four-dimensional leader—and you'll carry that capability with you when we begin discussing assessment in chapter 9. So as you continue to practice being aware, let me point out two additional benefits you should begin to realize.

First, greater awareness increases your ability to tune in to others. Simply stated, the sharper your awareness of yourself becomes, the better you will become at observing others.

You will pick up the language of their bodies as they sit around the conference table. You will not just listen to their thoughts but become curious about the thoughts behind their thoughts. You will be better attuned to their emotions and how those emotions manifest in their bodies in what they say and in what they might say or do next.

Finally, as you continue to gain mastery, you will be more curious about the substance of their spiritual core and what drives them. And you will become more adept as a leader—whether the people at the table are your executive team, your key suppliers, or prospective new clients.

I'm not suggesting you will suddenly have x-ray vision and be able to predict others' every move. We are all vulnerable to misinterpreting people's words or actions. But you will simply notice more, take in more data, ask better questions, and be in a better position to lead.

Greater awareness leads to greater influence. If there is a classic pattern I see with leaders at odds with a coworker, it is the amount of time and energy they put into noticing all that is "wrong" with the other person. They have a whole list of examples of the person's bad behavior, and then a whole other list of what they believe the other person is thinking or feeling based on that bad behavior.

Their observations and evaluations can be quite extensive. They conclude with some form of "How do I influence (manipulate) this person to behave the way I'd like them to?"

Now, I get it. Sometimes other people act like jerks. They're exhibiting unacceptable behavior that should not be tolerated, and they *do* need to change in some ways. Dealing with these situations is part of the normal course of leadership. But they generally compose the minority of our coworker conflicts. In most situations, we have more influence than we realize; we just need to shift our paradigm.

Here's what I ask leaders after they have gone on for five or ten minutes about their coworker who irritates them: "How are *you* showing up (in all four of your dimensions)?"

In asking that question, I am challenging them to shift their paradigm. Instead of pouring all their attention and energy into the other person's bad behavior and manipulating them to change, they must shift their attention and energy to the person they have 100 percent control over—themselves (figure 24).

Figure 24. I will have greater influence by directing my attention to the person over whom I have 100 percent control.

The more you master self-awareness, the better you will become at leading yourself; decreasing others' ability to bother or intimidate you; and gradually, over time, expanding your ability to influence others.

> When leaders complain to me that someone irritates them—someone is really pushing their buttons—I remind them, "It's your button! It belongs to you!"

When leaders complain to me that someone irritates them—someone is really pushing their buttons—I remind them, "It's *your* button! It belongs to you!"

Now that we have put all four dimensions together and better understand how they interact with one another, let's take our awareness a step further and examine our default dimension and how it can bring out the best and the worst in us.

KEY TAKEAWAYS

- Turning off autopilot and turning on awareness can feel a little awkward at first, but with time and repetition, it becomes second nature. This, in turn, helps me be better at self-leadership rather than simply reacting to my circumstances.

- "Extreme" situations, when I am either at my best or my worst, are the best times for awareness. In these situations, I am able to see each of my four dimensions more clearly.

- The diagram for the four dimensions, with an inner S (spiritual) surrounded by P (physical), I (intellectual), and E (emotional), is an intentional reminder of how the dimensions connect and interact with one another.

- Though it is concealed within the other three dimensions, my inner core spiritual dimension ultimately drives everything.

- The outer three dimensions—physical, intellectual, and emotional—represent my personality to others.

- To be at my best, I need to be strong and balanced in all four dimensions.

- All four dimensions "touch," or influence, one another.

- How I'm doing in my "tangible" physical dimension can be a strong indicator of how I'm doing in the other three dimensions.

- When I become more aware, I should immediately see opportunities to change.

- When I become more self-aware, it equips me to better tune in to, connect with, and lead others.

QUESTIONS FOR REFLECTION

- What new aspects are you noticing about yourself through increased self-awareness in all four of your dimensions?

- When is the last time you went through the awkward phase of learning to do something for the first time? What lessons does that offer as you learn to make turning off autopilot and turning on awareness more second nature?

- For the next four weeks (or whatever timeline you want), what routine do you want to have for practicing awareness of the four dimensions?

- What is one example where you have noticed something new in others as a result of noticing so much more in yourself?

- **Go to LeadLikeYouBook.com for additional exercises related to this chapter.**

CHAPTER 8
MY DEFAULT DIMENSION

Today you are You, that is truer than true.
There is no one alive who is Youer than You.
—Dr. Seuss

Learn how to see. Realize that everything con-
nects to everything else.
—Leonardo da Vinci

One spring, I was invited to join three leaders as they gathered
for a quarterly retreat. Dan, Sam, and Jon were dear friends
who had known one another since college. Today they run
different companies in different cities and have been meeting like this for several years. Much like a Young Presidents'
Organization forum, their agenda includes giving one another
updates on themselves and their companies, sharing progress
toward goals, and presenting one or two current challenges
they are facing for the group's input.

As they talked, I listened and observed—not only in the
formal sessions but also as we played golf, socialized, and
ate dinner. Our setting, at a beautiful hotel overlooking the
Atlantic Ocean, was relaxed and informal. These longtime

friends felt safe with one another. They seemed quick to let their guard down and be vulnerable.

But there were also moments when one would challenge another, introducing a little stress. One such difficult conversation carried on for the better part of a morning—leaving two of the leaders somewhat at odds with one another until later in the day. It is good when "iron sharpens iron," but it also hurts!

Reflecting on the time with these men as I flew home, I realized that each one of them operated with a distinctly different style—revealed in their presence, the types of questions they asked, how they processed data, and their strengths and weaknesses. As well-rounded as they were as leaders, they each had a default way of showing up—whether as an emotional-dimension "heart guy," an intellectual-dimension "head guy," or a physical-dimension "gut guy."

In this chapter, I'd like to introduce you to a higher level of self-awareness. I'll call this Awareness 2.0. Everything we have discussed up to this point is a prerequisite for Awareness 2.0: First, recognize how much you operate on autopilot (chapter 1). Second, pause the autopilot and tune in to all four dimensions of yourself: your outer physical, intellectual, and emotional dimensions, as well as your inner spiritual core self (chapters 2–6). And finally, understand how the four dimensions interact with one another to form an overall expression of your leadership (chapter 7).

In Awareness 2.0, we begin to see that we have a "default dimension." One of the outer three personality dimensions—physical, intellectual, or emotional—tends to be our go-to dimension, the one we tend to use the most and the one in which we feel strongest and safest.[31] By recognizing this dominant dimension, we can better understand our automatic ways of taking in information, making decisions, and leading others, and we gain greater insight about how this default mode both complements and clashes with the default dimensions of others.

THREE LEADERS, THREE DEFAULT DIMENSIONS

Think about whether your default dimension might be physical, intellectual, or emotional, and then see if you identify with one of these three leaders.

Dan, the "Heart Guy"

Dan was the most outgoing of the bunch. In fact, if you spent a few hours with Dan, you might feel like his best friend. He seemed to have a way of reading me and always said just the right thing to make me feel comfortable and welcome. He was witty, quick with a funny story, and not only made all of us laugh but had a big laugh himself.

As CEO of a boutique investment banking firm, Dan had a lot of irons in the fire. He worked crazy hours and seemed to have so much going on that it was actually hard to keep up with his many ventures. At the beginning of the weekend, I was impressed by Dan's apparent success. But as the conversations continued, I began to notice a lack of self-confidence in Dan. Making himself vulnerable, he said he was unsure about the next steps to take on several of his key projects. He was worried about "how it would look" to the market if he didn't close a pending deal. Also, one of the other guys challenged him at one point over exaggerating the likelihood of one of his larger deals going through. Apparently, exaggeration was a trait of Dan's that had been discussed in the past. And when that conflict arose between the other two guys, Dan's response was to get quiet and pull back from the fray.

Sam, the "Head Guy"

Sam struck me from the beginning as very likable and trustworthy. He didn't dominate conversations as much as the other two, but when he did speak, he was thoughtful and offered valuable insights. Sam ran a strategy consulting firm with clients across the country, and you could tell he was good at thinking about the future and how to best be prepared for it. Whereas Jon, the "gut guy," would be quick to offer *the* solution, Sam tended to see a range of options, each with varying levels of risk and potential success. And he tended to process things based more on facts than on feelings. Like Dan, Sam seemed to be having a lot of success in his practice. And yet I was struck by the fact that, when it came time to consider his own strategies for growing his business, he seemed hesitant. He viewed many of the obstacles for his business with trepidation and self-doubt; despite his past and present success, he was worried about his future.

Jon, the "Gut Guy"

The first impression I had of Jon was literally a physical one. He was taller than my six feet, had a firm handshake and a strong chin, and appeared ready to deal with (and dominate!) anything that might come across his path. He was not quite as outgoing as Dan but likable enough. If anything, he seemed to be sizing me up and drawing his own conclusions about me. Jon was president of a five-thousand-plus-employee firm that was very labor intensive, and I could easily picture him out in the field addressing his troops in a strong voice. Not much seemed to scare Jon, and he had ably piloted his company through the recent economic downturn, emerging with a larger market share and strong profits.

In this group setting with his two friends, I noticed Jon seemed quickest to diagnose what a given problem was—and to tell us his recommended solution. At times, when the conversation became a little more tense, he would talk over the others, occasionally with little verbal jabs. Jon was one of the two who got sideways with each other, strongly resisting Sam's analysis of a challenge he was facing. Jon said that Sam was "putting him in a box," and he didn't like it! By the end of the weekend, I felt I had earned Jon's respect and trust. We ended up having some one-on-one conversations where he shared with me about his marriage and the ways he wanted it to be better. For being the guy who most intimidated me at the beginning of the weekend, I felt that Jon was the one who opened up and was ultimately the most vulnerable and real of the three.

Dan, Sam, and Jon represent the three different leadership styles—heart (emotional), head (intellectual), and gut (physical)—that show up in my coaching work.[32] Now, I am not putting people in boxes. No two leaders are alike. Everyone has their own "leadership DNA," a unique combination of method, style, and energy they bring to their role. And yes, we all have the potential to operate in one or more of the three dimensions at any given time. But if you pay attention, you will find that you tend to revert to one dimension as your default, especially under pressure.

Out of all the chapters in my book, this one may be the most helpful to you. The majority of leaders with whom I have shared this Awareness 2.0 framework over the years have certainly found it to be so. On the other hand, you might be one who pushes back. You may find it too confining or formulaic. I encourage you to be curious and see if parts of this framework indeed could be helpful to you, at least some of the time.

GREATEST STRENGTH, GREATEST WEAKNESS

While all leaders possess a heart (emotional dimension), head (intellectual dimension), and gut (physical dimension), they tend to favor, and lead from, one of these dimensions more than the other two. This is the leader's default dimension.

Before we explore your default dimension, I need to introduce you to a powerful concept that, as soon as you grasp its implications, will help you lead more effectively. Here it is: your greatest strengths and your greatest weaknesses are wrapped around the same thing—a common characteristic. The characteristics that produce your greatest strengths as a leader, the unique abilities that result in your greatest successes, and the talents that set you apart from others are the same characteristics that produce your greatest weaknesses, the obstacles that hold you back, and the situations that sabotage or derail your progress (figure 25).

> Your greatest strengths and your greatest weaknesses are wrapped around the same thing.

Let that sink in.

Figure 25. Your great strength and great weakness are related to a common characteristic.

If I asked you to identify the top one or two strengths that make you so good at what you do, what would you say they are? Be as specific as possible. What comes to mind immediately?

Now, answer these questions: What happens when you overuse that strength? When you engage it *all* the time? When you apply it to every single person or problem you encounter? When your strength is a hammer and you believe everything is a nail? Our greatest strength becomes our greatest weakness when we indiscriminately apply it in all situations.

Let me give you an example that my wife and kids could tell you about me. If you haven't figured it out already, I tend to be a "head" guy. My default dimension is the intellectual. As a result, one of my strengths is the ability to plan ahead. I am almost always prepared for what comes next. I do this by consciously and subconsciously thinking about the future. I constantly scan my environment or my schedule for threats or roadblocks. Where I anticipate problems, I design solutions to deal with those problems ahead of time. It's a strength that enables me to show up steady and ready. I have everything planned out! (See figure 26.)

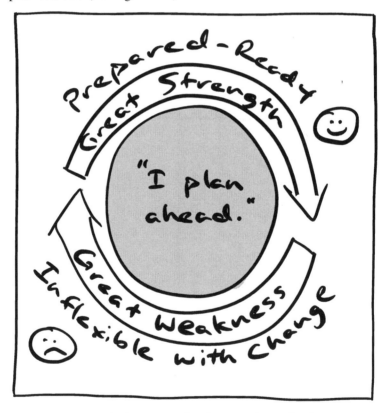

Figure 26. One example of great strength and great weakness related to a common characteristic.

So what happens when Marta suggests on Thursday that we do something different as a family Saturday morning—when I have had my personal plans in place for Saturday morning for several days now?! My immediate instinct is to say no. To protest. Even to get angry. She's messing with my perfectly planned future. Though I have gotten better over time, this sort of automatic, autopilot reaction still happens more often than I would like to admit.

Do you see the link between my strength and my weakness? I can plan things out so well that it inhibits flexibility and spontaneity. I can have it so together personally that it creates conflict interpersonally. I can be in the future so much that I am never in the present.

Maybe you see a comparable link between your strength and weakness, or maybe it's still not connecting for you. When I first bring up this concept, most leaders nod their heads in knowing agreement. They intuitively know their greatest strengths and greatest weaknesses are related; they just haven't yet figured out how this connection applies in their lives. I assure you they are quite clear by the time we finish our coaching work together. And it should become a little clearer to you as you begin to understand your default dimension.

Here's the biggest problem with not understanding how your greatest strength and greatest weakness are related: you will keep repeating the great weakness, because you will keep manifesting that characteristic that is also the source of your greatest strength.

Let's take a more in-depth look at the three default dimensions. One of these should resonate with you more than the other two. Which one is it?

THE HEART LEADER

Heart leaders, or leaders who default to the emotional dimension, navigate life by feelings: "How will this make me feel?" "How will others feel about this decision?" "How do I feel about how others feel?" They are very sensitive to the people around them and know just what to do and say to win over their audience. But if they are not careful, they will be so tuned in to the feelings of others for their validation, identity, and direction that they will have difficulty tuning in to themselves, listening to their own voice, and following their own compass.

When Heart Leaders Are at Their Best

Heart leaders perform! They rise to the top because they accomplish, achieve, and meet or exceed others' expectations. They are people pleasers in all the good ways. They excel at sensing what makes others happy, and then work hard to give them what they want—whether they are selling something, delivering a speech, or reporting quarterly results to their boards. Heart-based leaders tend to be witty and highly relational, and they enjoy settings where they meet and mix with others. Heart leaders have the following attributes:

- **They inspire others to do great things.** Heart leaders are charismatic individuals who motivate others toward the same high standards of excellence and accomplishment that they expect of themselves. And they know what it takes to inspire a wide variety of followers.

- **They know what will "sell."** Whether it's an idea or a product, heart leaders easily figure out what their audience wants, and then how to promote and deliver it in a way so that it will be bought. This characteristic accounts for the many CEOs who reach the top following successful stints in marketing or sales.

What Is Really Going On

The heart leader has determined that the way to get ahead in life is to accomplish and please others.[33] To do this, these leaders develop a highly sensitive radar to tune in to the body language, feelings, and opinions of everyone around them. Somewhere deep inside, they contend with feelings of shame and inadequacy; most feel their worth comes from performing—doing, not simply "being." This makes it hard for them to rest and be still. Many become workaholics, for they could always be doing more to please more people. And this is why efficiency is so important to them: "If I can do two or three things at once, that makes me two to three times more valuable!"

One of the ironies about unhealthy heart leaders is that many are actually quite disconnected from their own hearts. They can be far more attuned to the feelings of others than to their own feelings. While they appear to be sensitive or sympathetic, for many it is an act—simply a way they have learned to behave to endear themselves to others. When you ask them what emotion—their own emotion—they are feeling in the moment, they have a hard time answering.

Caution! When Heart Leaders Are Vulnerable

Especially under pressure, heart leaders may do anything, ranging from simple exaggeration to outright deceit, to appear successful and make you like them. When I read about a CEO of a large corporation indicted for fraud or corruption, I wonder what drove this leader to it and how much of it had to do with keeping up the appearance of being successful. Over the years, I have known heart leaders who lived a pantomime of success—a beautiful home, luxury automobiles, fabulous trips, and kids in private schools—while dancing on the edge of bankruptcy.

Despite being highly "relational," many heart leaders, especially at the tops of organizations, don't have any close friends. Oh, they have lots of "friends"—golfing buddies or drinking buddies, for example—but none they allow into the inner sanctum of their own doubts, vulnerabilities, or dreams.

One of the areas I so often end up working on with heart leaders is their self-confidence. I'll never forget the early months of getting to know a CEO in Boston. This guy oozed success. He was cofounder of a technology company that, after a few years, was doing about $100 million in sales. He regularly vetted requests to be the keynote speaker at industry conferences and had a book coming out soon from a major publisher. At one of our first meetings, he walked in and dropped a magazine in front of me with his face on the cover. Accomplishments—check! Success—check! And yet what was the central challenge in his leadership that emerged for us to address in our work together? How to have, speak, and act with greater self-confidence. You see, heart leaders can be so good at tuning in to the voices of others, and yet they have great difficulty listening to their own voices—the yin and yang of their greatest strength and their greatest weakness.

As heart leaders rise through the ranks, their vulnerability to their shadow side, if not addressed, leads to more and more dysfunction. Specifically, I have observed the following maladies most frequently among CEOs who default to their heart (emotional) dimension:

- **They change their minds frequently.** One executive will give his or her input to the CEO. The

CEO makes a decision, and the executive walks out, thinking things are final. The next day, the executive learns the CEO has changed his or her mind since meeting with another executive. And so on.

- **They avoid conflict.** Because heart leader CEOs want to be liked, they have difficulty confronting problems, delivering bad news, and holding people accountable. Instead, they ignore problems and hope, somehow, they will get better, or they try to delegate their "dirty work" to others.

- **They can be preoccupied with image.** People can sense when unhealthy heart leaders are consumed with building their own brand image— "She has such a big ego!" These same leaders are vulnerable to building companies that look good from the outside but lack true value or are incredibly dysfunctional internally.

THE HEAD LEADER

Leaders who default to their intellect are analytical in their decision making. More so than heart and gut leaders, head leaders will see a whole range of options on the path ahead, and logic will be their guide in choosing from them. They are the smart ones among us who love to take in data and make meaning out of it all. Always looking to the future, they have an innate ability to sniff out risk; strategy comes easy for them. But they can overdo the analysis to the point of planning and planning and never taking action.

When Head Leaders Are at Their Best

Head leaders are smart and prepared. They achieve by thinking things through and then harnessing the complementary strengths of a team to take action. These leaders are always contemplating what comes next and preparing accordingly. They organize and create systems to manage activities and hold people accountable.

When things are murky, head leaders have the patience to sort through the confusion, prioritize, and determine the best path forward. They are practical and unencumbered by emotions in their decision making. While others are talking, head leaders are often listening; when they finally speak, it is often with words of wisdom. Not only can they act with courage personally, but they encourage others to act as well. Head leaders tend to possess the following attributes:

- **They are superb at risk management.** Because they are always thinking ahead and contemplating the future, head leaders excel at anticipating where ambushes and breakdowns could occur and developing plans to mitigate such risks.[34]

- **They are visionary and strategic.** At their best, head leaders can envision the future with great clarity, as well as the strategic steps necessary to make that imagined future a reality. They are great at seeing how to integrate different pieces of the puzzle.

- **They are trustworthy.** Because of their ability to anticipate and manage risk and change, resourceful head leaders project their sense of inner guidance and stability outward, enabling them to gain the trust of others quickly.

What Is Really Going On

The head leader somehow learned early on that the world can be an unpredictable and dangerous place.[35] The best way to deal with such unpredictability is to fully anticipate all that could go wrong and prepare accordingly. Whereas the heart leader's radar innately senses other people's feelings, the head leader's radar is finely tuned to anticipate all that could happen on the path ahead. Thus, in both healthy and unhealthy ways, head leaders live in the future. Such leaders, when "lost in their thoughts," are not present.[36]

The head leader's emotional companion is most often some degree of fear. Whereas we usually think of the heart as the metaphorical home of our emotions, I often refer to fear as an emotion of the head. Fear, as we defined it in chapter 5, pertains to the future: "What I want could be taken away from me." The only way to process fear is by "imagining" what could happen, and this imagining takes place in the leader's head.

Caution! When Head Leaders Are Vulnerable

Head leaders often get promoted for their smarts—having the best ideas, framing problems so they can be solved, seeing the big picture, or simply always speaking words of wisdom just when they are needed. Their great challenge, however, is in having the courage to put their ideas into action. No action, no results.

I remember a past CEO of a think tank who fits the head leader description. How's that for an appropriate role? Michael was an articulate communicator, well organized, and always prepared. He had clear command of all the facts and information that went into developing and communicating policy, and he organized his company so that it delivered good products and decent profits.

But Michael let his fear and anxieties get the best of him. Though no one in the organization under him saw it, he constantly barraged his board with scenarios of impending danger to the company. He also barraged them with lengthy emails he expected them to read as a context for his concerns. Board members who would actually read the memorandums, including the board chair, consistently concluded that his fears were overblown and that they interfered with his taking action on more pressing issues.

All the while, Michael complained, "They just don't get it!" Eventually, after about a year of sparring back and forth, the board chair asked for his resignation. A new CEO was appointed, and the company continued on successfully.

As smart head leaders take on increasing levels of responsibility, they need to recognize their vulnerability to being controlled by emotions of fear and worry. And they must adapt their leadership away from an overreliance on "thinking." Leaders I have worked with in this category often self-sabotage in the following ways:

- **They analyze, and analyze some more.** The unhealthy head leader believes "If I just had a little more information, I would know exactly what to do and would have a plan for every contingency." They depend overly on data and logic, and they fail to take into account their own gut instincts.

- **They get paralyzed.** The head leader's tendency to worry so much can make them overly cautious and hesitant to take action. They often have plenty of information with which to take action but fail to act.

- **They distance themselves from others.** Under stress and probably fearful, the head leader can withdraw into endless cycles of thought, believing he or she alone must think the way out of a problem. Precisely at the time when teamwork could help develop solutions, this leader distances him- or herself from others who could help the most.

THE GUT LEADER

Leaders who operate mostly from their physical dimension, their gut, know just what to do. And they do it quickly. Their decision matrix is simple—they view their options as black or white.

Unlike head leaders, who gather and analyze a whole slew of alternatives, or heart leaders, who must take into account all the ways they, and others, will feel about the decision, gut leaders tend to consider just the polarities of an issue: Is it good or bad? Fair or unfair? Go or no-go? And their goals are simple as well; they want to win and dominate. But they can get into trouble with their binary view of people and situations, and alienate their teammates with their constant striving to win arguments.

When Gut Leaders Are at Their Best

With a clarity on what needs to get done, gut leaders stay focused on the goal and are not easily distracted by the challenges that lie between. In fact, the challenge of overcoming obstacles can energize them.

Their strength and conviction inspire others to follow them. And while some are intimidated by their blunt, straight-talking manner, followers of gut leaders always know where they stand. Gut leaders tend to have the following attributes:

- **They have no fear!** When operating from their gut, these leaders move ahead with courage and strength, unencumbered with their own fears or the feelings of others. They inspire others to follow them into battle.

- **Their communication is clear and unambiguous.** Operating by instinct, gut leaders see things clearly and communicate so that others know exactly where they stand.

- **They take care of others.** Gut leaders, with a clear sense of what is just and fair, will look out for others, especially those they view as weaker or disadvantaged. They provide protection and shelter, and their actions can rise to the level of heroic.[37]

What Is Really Going On

Gut leaders roll out of bed every day ready to do battle. Life is indeed a contact sport, and they suit up in their protective armor, ready to engage and win. Somewhere in their formative years, they learned that the world is hostile and threatening, and the best defense is to always be on offense. At risk of losing touch with their true identities in their interior spiritual dimension, they constantly fortify their exteriors. They will protect themselves at any cost, generally by attacking anything or anyone that threatens to control them or take away their power. The problem with wearing a heavy coat of armor is that you lose sensitivity to when you bump into, or step on, others around you.

Gut leaders navigate with some degree of anger, even if it is just an undercurrent of frustration. When resourceful, they channel this anger in healthy ways: they fix things that are broken, they correct mistakes, and if they are losing, they figure out how to win fast. When not resourceful, they vent their anger at others, at a minimum irritating others and at worst being a bully.

Caution! When Gut Leaders Are Vulnerable

As with leaders who default to their hearts or their heads, gut leaders most often get into trouble when they overdo a good thing, turning their greatest strengths into their greatest weaknesses. They are strong and powerful. But what happens when they are strong and powerful all the time?

I had breakfast one morning with a gut leader whose company had lost two employees in the past two months—one to a heart attack, and another to a ravaging return of cancer. What do his employees and those two families need from this tough leader at such a time? Tenderness. Gentleness. A patient, listening ear.

And what happens for the rapid-fire gut leader who sees everything as an either-or, black-and-white problem? They can just as easily make rapid-fire poor decisions when they fail to recognize the solution might lie somewhere in the middle.

Hard-charging gut leaders risk isolating themselves when they have no one in their inner circle strong enough to tell them their breath stinks. Ruling with an iron fist, they snuff out creativity and the complementary skills others could bring. Oh yes, they get results but often at the cost of alienating others who suffer in silence or finally decide to take their talents elsewhere. Here are some of the more common vulnerabilities aware gut leaders share with me:

- **They intimidate and antagonize.** Without even opening their mouths, gut leaders can have an intimidating physical presence. And once they talk, telling others exactly how they feel, they can easily rub those around them the wrong way.

- **They have difficulty navigating the gray.** Not all decision making is black and white. Some decisions require leaders to navigate the gray. This can threaten a gut leader, tempting them to avoid the decision or downplay its importance.

- **They can go in the wrong direction fast.** These leaders can take speedy and decisive action—in the wrong direction! They can quickly jump to conclusions on matters that demand a little more thought (head) or sensitivity (heart).

- **They're looking for someone to be against.** The competitive gut leader is always looking for a sparring partner, someone they can pick on as a demonstration of their strength in front of others. Itching for a fight in a group setting, they will single out their victim.

YOUR DEFAULT DIMENSION

Which of these descriptions most resonates with you? Do you see yourself in any of them? Can you identify the default dimension of others close to you?

Again, we are not trying to put people in boxes. We all possess a heart, a head, and a gut. All three dimensions are available to all of us at all times. And, as we will learn later, we are all at our best if we are routinely using all three as we lead. But generally, one will emerge as our default or dominant dimension—when we are either at our best or at our worst.

We have spent the bulk of our time up to now expanding your vision of what it means to be aware as a leader:

- We have taken the vague notion of self-awareness and broken it down into four distinct dimensions.

- Each of these four dimensions holds deeper layers of awareness to be considered.

- The four dimensions are interdependent and affect one another.

- And finally, we have become aware that we usually have one dimension to which we default— both when we are at our best and at our worst as a leader.

I have devoted two-thirds of the book to self-awareness— for good reason. If you can become significantly more self-aware, you're two-thirds of the way to becoming a better leader!

But being more aware does not by itself make you a better leader. I can be very aware that I am overweight and need to lose fifty pounds. But awareness alone will not help me lose the fifty pounds. Another way I express this with my leaders is that change begins with awareness, but awareness alone does not equal change.

We now need to build on this newfound awareness to become a better, more effective leader. To do that we turn to part 2. In the next two chapters, you will learn how to assess whether a given dimension is serving you well, and then how to adjust so your four dimensions are strong, balanced, and enabling you to lead with your best self.

KEY TAKEAWAYS

- My greatest strength and greatest weakness tend to be wrapped around a common characteristic. Until I recognize this, and because I want to keep exercising the greatest strength, I will keep repeating my greatest weakness.

- I, like everyone, have a heart (the emotional dimension), head (the intellectual dimension), and gut (the physical dimension). With time, I may begin to be aware that I spend more time in one of these than the others—making it my default dimension.

- If my default is to lead with my (emotional) heart, I navigate a lot by feelings, often the feelings of others. My default emotion is likely shame.

    - My strengths may include inspiring others to do great things and knowing what will "sell" and how to sell it.

    - My weaknesses may include changing my mind frequently, avoiding conflict or difficult conversations, and being preoccupied with my image.

- If my default is to lead with my (intellectual) head, I rely heavily on my intellect, analysis, and logic. My default emotion is fear.

  - My strengths may include being excellent at anticipating and managing risk, being visionary and strategic, and quickly earning others' trust.

  - My weaknesses may include overanalyzing a problem, getting paralyzed and being slow to take action, and distancing myself from others.

- If my default is to lead with my (physical) gut, I navigate by simple gut instinct, which presents my options in black and white. My default emotion is anger.

  - My strengths may include taking action with strength and courage, communicating in a way that is direct and clear, and taking care of others.

  - My weaknesses may include intimidating and antagonizing others, having difficulty navigating the gray, and always looking for someone to be against.

QUESTIONS FOR REFLECTION

- What are your top one or two strengths that make you so good at what you do?

- What happens when you overuse that strength? When you insist on engaging it *all* the time? When you apply it to every single person or problem you encounter? Is it possible it becomes one of your greatest weaknesses?

- Which of the three dimensions—heart, head, or gut—resonates most for you? Which resonates the least?

- **Go to LeadLikeYouBook.com for additional exercises related to this chapter.**

PART 2

ASSESS AND ADJUST

CHAPTER 9

ASSESS

Count what is countable, measure what is measurable. What is not measurable, make measurable.

—Galileo Galilei

If you can measure it, you can manage it.

—Original author unknown

I came to the meeting expecting to talk about the leader's future. Instead, I found him stuck in his past.

Jim had sent me an email a few days before our meeting telling me that he wanted to talk through his plans for the future expansion of his company. But when we sat down that Monday afternoon, I could immediately see he wasn't in a mood to talk about the future of anything.

"Rob, I'm not good. And I don't really know why."

He continued: "I've been working hard and getting a lot done, but there's something bugging me, and I can't figure out what it is. And no, I'm not in a frame of mind to talk about our future strategy today. I need to figure out how to get myself to a better place for the rest of this week."

I had been working with Jim for several months, and his self-awareness had grown significantly in that time. With my prompting, he immediately began taking inventory of himself using the four dimensions (see chapter 7).

But this time, I had him do something new. At the end of his awareness inventory for each dimension, I had him pause before moving on to the next dimension. In that pause, I asked him to give himself an overall grade for that dimension based on his self-awareness list. I suggested he use a one-to-ten scale, "with ten being at your best and one being you don't know how you got out of bed this morning!"

Table 5 captures his self-assessment.

Dimension	Self-Awareness	Overall Assessment
Physical	Tired, weak posture, tense face, and moving at a fast pace	6
Intellectual	A thousand thoughts, staffing issues, positive thoughts in general, and proud of himself for finally letting an executive go	9–10
Emotional	Glad in general, although a little sad about comments someone made to him last week	6
Spiritual	Feeling very connected to his core identity and purpose and having a deeper sense that the future is bright	9

Table 5. Jim's self-awareness and assessment.

When he was done, and without giving any feedback of my own, I asked him, "Do you see anything new?"

"Oh yeah!"

I grinned, curious and very interested to hear his answer.

"The physical and the emotional. They go together—both a 6. And I know why! That negative comment someone made to me last week—I've been trying to forget about it. But it left me feeling like I wasn't working as hard as I should. And, without noticing [autopilot!], I cranked up my work, grinding all through the weekend with no breaks. Getting triggered emotionally led me to work nonstop and wear myself out."

Self-assessing—simply assigning a value to all that he noticed—revealed new insights that self-awareness alone could not.

THE IMPORTANCE OF ASSESSMENT

Every day as a leader, you are assessing. Consciously or unconsciously, you continuously measure and judge how the areas under your responsibility are doing:

- Inventory is higher than usual.
- Sales are exceeding quota this quarter.
- Our profit margin is too low.
- His marketing pitch is boring and doesn't persuade.
- Hiring is ahead of schedule.

And why do you assess constantly? Because your job as a leader is to be sure that everything under your control is at its best, or on its way to being at its best.

Generally, people and processes don't automatically move toward an optimal state on their own. That is why we need leaders like you. And you need clarity on what "best" looks like, how far away we are from "best," and what we need to do to close the gap toward "best." This is assessment (figure 27).

Figure 27. Assessment measures the gap between present state and optimal state.

Think about your particular areas of responsibility and accountability. What would happen if you never paused to assess how things are going? What if you just let everything run on autopilot?

I think you can see pretty quickly that you would become irrelevant as a leader. Machines maintain. Managers maintain. But leaders assess to determine "How are we doing now compared to our goals?" and "How do we need to change things to ensure we meet or exceed our goals?"

And so it is with leading yourself. You must continuously assess yourself to know your current leadership condition and know how it compares to you at your best.

Another great leadership tool I picked up as an Army officer was the after-action review (AAR). This is a team debrief after a major activity. Following every leadership "event," whether it is a morning training session on the gunnery range, an overnight recon patrol, or a two-week tactical field exercise, leaders gather and do an AAR. The AAR is an assessment:

- What happened?
- What went well?
- What did not go well?
- What actions led to what outcomes?
- What will we pay more attention to or do differently next time?

No book learning can replace this type of real-world, real-people, real-actions evaluation. And the same is true for you when you pause to assess.

> No one can assess you at your
> best better than you can.

What Are We Assessing?

What is "your best"? Because every leader is different, "best" will be different for every leader.

You have your own way of gathering information, making decisions, connecting with people, expressing your thoughts, showing up, feeling, and influencing others. Some days you do these things poorly, some days you do them really well, and many days you are somewhere in between.

Though you may want me, or someone else, to define what is "best" for you, that would be impossible. No one can know you as well as you know you. And no one can assess you at your best better than you can.

And guess what? With time and progress, your best probably changes as you stretch yourself and discover you can do and be more than you thought possible. So there's no ideal standard for what makes the best leader, and anyone who says there is, is mostly describing the standard that worked best for them!

So how do we use assessment in our pursuit to be the best version of ourselves? To assess is to judge something, to determine the amount present, or to calculate value. For our purposes, once we are aware of ourselves fully, in all four dimensions, we then assess to assign a value to our current condition—individually in each dimension and then cumulatively in all four—to assess our overall condition to lead. Our ultimate goal, as we will discuss later, is to be *strong* in each dimension and *balanced* across all four dimensions.

How Do We Assess?

How do you assess your team? What metrics do you use? If you are a sales leader, I doubt you would get very far by reporting that year-to-date sales are "so-so." If you lead operations, reporting that your plant in North Carolina is "pretty good" wouldn't cut it with the CEO. And if you are the CFO, an income statement that says revenue this quarter is "bad" would lead to a whole lot more questions.

Such assessments are vague, subject to interpretation, and difficult to compare from one time period to another. Instead, we measure with specific, known units that are meaningful in the moment and over time.

The sales leader reports "gross sales revenue" or "number of contracts closed." The operations leader measures the North

Carolina plant as having "97.3 percent uptime last month." And the CFO better summarizes by reporting "net income was down 2 percent compared to last year."

In the same way, when you assess yourself in each of the four dimensions, you will want to measure as specifically as possible and in a way that will be useful over time.

Beyond those guidelines, you should feel free to use whatever scale is most meaningful to you. Here are some of the most common examples I see leaders use when assessing themselves in each of the dimensions:

- percentage scale: 1 to 100 percent
- number scale: 1 to 10, or 1 to 5, or –10 to +10 (with 0 being average)
- letter scale: A, B, C, D, F
- color scale: green (good), yellow (caution), red (bad)

Use a scale that resonates with you. Assigning values or grades will feel somewhat subjective at first. But with repetition and consistency, your assessments will become more objective. You will recognize what 75 percent in your physical dimension looks and feels like. Or you will know when you are at a B+ emotionally.

BASIC ASSESSMENT: HOW AM I DOING RIGHT NOW?

🖊 **"JOURNAL TIME"**

Go to LeadLikeYouBook.com for an exercise related to this assessment.

Let's look at an example of Mark as he pauses to (1) be aware and then (2) assess during his drive to the office. The prompts for each dimension can be found in chapter 7.

Physical

As he heads to the office Monday morning, Mark reviews his prompts for the physical dimension. He is aware of the following:

- He didn't get much extra rest over the weekend, and he's feeling a bit tired as the week kicks off.

- He struggled to complete a tough CrossFit workout at 6:00 a.m. that morning, though he has been sticking with his three-times-per-week schedule.

- His eating and drinking were not great over the weekend—a little too much of each at a party Saturday night and again watching the game Sunday afternoon. He still feels the effects of overindulging in his gut.

- He continues to notice tension in his shoulders and neck to the point where he frequently tries to loosen them up.

Overall, Mark doesn't feel as fresh and light on his feet as he would like for a Monday morning. On a scale of 1 to 10, he assesses himself at a 6 physically.

Intellectual

Mark reviews the prompts for his intellectual dimension and is aware of the following:

- Foremost on his mind are two things: (1) a presentation deck he needs to complete for tomorrow's board meeting, which could be contentious, and (2) a phone call this afternoon with the president of a major client company who is threatening to pull his business. Mark has several other meetings and phone calls planned for the day, but these are the two events he's thinking about the most.

- Mark also notices he is still thinking back to a conversation he had with his wife yesterday about their daughter and her first week at college. Both of them are concerned about her making friends and not feeling lonely. He caught himself strategizing on whom he knew he could reach out to regarding his daughter.

- As he thinks about the client call this afternoon, Mark realizes he feels unprepared to make a convincing argument for the client president to not switch vendors. He needs more information from his senior vice presidents of sales and product design to make sure his company can follow through with what he wants to tell the client he will do.

- Finally, Mark checks in with what he is thinking about himself. Overall, he notices he is thinking,

"I have so much to do today and this week, I am not sure I can do it all really well."

Mark realizes the most dangerous thing about his intellectual dimension right now is that he is beating himself up mentally for being "unprepared." He assesses himself as a 5. "Wow! That's no way to start the day," he quickly thinks to himself.

Emotional

Mark is glad just to be assessing where he is emotionally. Historically, this is not something he is used to, but he has discovered it to be so helpful. "After all," he remembers, "if I am not noticing my emotions, they are probably controlling me, and that can be dangerous!" The emotional prompts lead him to be aware of the following:

- Frustration is the feeling that comes up first. He is frustrated that his calendar is so full in light of his not being completely prepared for all his meetings and calls. He realizes that he directs this frustration at both himself and his assistant for filling his calendar and not leaving enough prep time in between. Almost as quickly, he notices the tension in his shoulders as he feels this emotion in his body. He relaxes a little in response and reminds himself that, if he is not careful, he could take out his frustration on his assistant when he first sees her at the office.

- Staying with his emotional assessment a little longer, he also recognizes he misses his daughter. He feels a dose of sadness that she is no longer at home, but at the same time, he is glad that she is at college where she belongs. Truly, he has mixed emotions here.

Again, Mark is glad to notice his emotions and the effect they could have on how he enters the office. He gives himself a 7 in this dimension. He's generally in good shape but needs to stay aware so the undercurrent of tension doesn't lead him to lose his temper.

Spiritual

As Mark moves to the spiritual prompts, he remembers that this dimension can be the toughest area to remain aware of, but that when he stays with it, it helps him be stronger in all three of the other dimensions as well. He notices the following:

- As usual, when he assesses this dimension, Mark first reflects on his identity and his roles as husband to Sarah and father to Emily, John, and Jacob. This awareness actually serves to settle him down as he connects with the purpose for which he works so hard. He is providing for the four of them, but he wants his identity to be more than just that of a good provider; he wants to be a great partner to his wife and a great father to his kids.

- Next, Mark goes to his purpose in founding his company. He wants to provide an excellent product that will make people's lives better, and he wants to do it working with people he enjoys being around. It reminds him to ask himself, "Would I want to work around me?!" The tension and frustration he has been feeling have led to some curt replies and feeling too busy to be really

present with some of his executives who have
wanted more time with him.

- Finally, Mark assesses for consistency between
  his inner spiritual dimension and the other three
  external dimensions. This exercise helps him to
  recenter and reconnect with his identity as "a
  man of good character who lives each day seeking
  to help others."

As he was first assessing his spiritual dimension, Mark
probably would have given himself a 4 or 5, largely because,
as usual when operating purely on autopilot, he was disconnected from it. But the mere discipline of assessing led to some
immediate minor adjustments (which we'll cover in detail
in the next chapter) that now have him at more of a 7 or 8.
Further meditation and reflection could bring that number
even higher.

Readiness to Lead

Before finishing his morning assessment ritual, Mark adds it
all up and assesses his overall readiness to lead (table 6).

Mark gives himself an overall score of 7 in terms of his
readiness to lead. This is a snapshot based on how he's doing
during his drive to the office. He knows he will be functional
and get things done as a 7 leader. But he sure would like to
function more like a 9 or 10. That would be Mark at his best!

Use this basic assessment anytime, anywhere. Two critical
times are at the beginning of your day and just before a really
important meeting, conversation, or presentation. Remember,
you're not going to be at your best if you enter your day or an
important event on autopilot. Tuning in and being self-aware

are the only ways you have a chance of making any necessary adjustments to be at your best.

Dimension	Self-Awareness	Overall Assessment
Physical	I am tired, my CrossFit workout was hard, I ate and drank too much, my gut's too full, and my shoulders and neck are tense.	6
Intellectual	I have a presentation for the board meeting (that could be tough!), I need more information to help a major client, and my daughter is starting college; can I do all this well?	5
Emotional	I am frustrated at having too much to do, sad because I miss my daughter, but I am glad she is at college.	7
Spiritual	I am husband to Sarah and father to Emily, John, and Jacob. I am a provider. I want to be a good husband and father and lead a good company, good people, and a good product. My outer three dimensions and my inner spiritual dimension are consistent with one another.	7–8
	My overall readiness to lead	7

Table 6. Mark's self-assessment and readiness to lead.

In the next chapter, we'll look at adjustments Mark, you, or any leader can make, both short term and longer term, to lead at your best.

TRENDLINE ASSESSMENTS: HOW AM I DOING OVER TIME?

It was August when I wrote this chapter. And I was reminded of a conversation I had with a CEO client toward the end of summer seven or eight years ago. Let's call him Ted. Ted and

I had been working together for about a year and a half, and we regularly employed the four-dimensional leadership framework in our coaching. He had made a lot of progress in his self-development as a leader.

But on this particular day, during this particular phone call, Ted was not doing well. It was summertime, and Ted had taken an extended vacation. Nearly two months had passed since our last call. I had expected to hear a report of resting and reflection. Instead, as soon as he got on the phone, Ted's first words were "Rob, the last seven weeks have *not* been good. I am totally out of whack!" In fact, things were so out of control for him personally that he was struggling to be calm, centered, and strong in leading his company.

So I said to Ted, "Let's rewind the game tape and see what happened over the past seven weeks that led to this state you find yourself in—'out of whack.'"

I had him take a sheet of paper and draw out a timeline. On the horizontal axis, he plotted, left to right across the page, the seven weeks. On a vertical axis on the left side of the paper, he created a scale ranging from "negative" (below the line) up to "good" (above the line). The midway point, at the horizontal line, he labeled "par," for average.

Then, beginning with the first week, Ted plotted his own assessment of how he was doing at the time, using P, I, E, and S as shorthand for the four dimensions. Take a look at Ted's chart in figure 28.

In the first week, notice that Ted started the seven-week stretch at a very good place. Physically, intellectually, emotionally, and spiritually, he was strong.

In the second week, physically, Ted began to decline a bit, which he attributed to "food"—eating the wrong kinds of it and eating too much. I, E, and S declined a little but still remained relatively high; P was the trigger that started the downward trajectory.

In the third week, the first of one of his two vacation weeks, Ted really dropped physically, again with the wrong diet of food and less sleep. Spiritually, he scored himself going into negative territory as well, with "no Bible" meditation and "no alone time"—both staples for him. Emotionally, he declined to average. Intellectually, he was still in good territory, reading a business book that he found very stimulating. But his intellectual dimension was not enough to stem the decline. In sum, assessing all four dimensions, Ted was now "out of whack."

In the fourth week, Ted's wife was injured in a boating accident. Giving much of his attention to her ("selflessness"), he "really stepped up" emotionally. But the attention required to manage his family during this difficult time kept him sub-par in his physical and spiritual dimensions.

In the fifth to seventh week, Ted struggled on, though he stayed mentally sharp. A second freakish boating incident involving a cousin threatened to knock him further off balance. But he was glad that, through it all, he had stayed in control emotionally, avoiding the angry outbursts he had been known for in the past. Still, he continued to be off balance physically and emotionally, leading to his "out of whack" assessment when he got on the phone with me.

Having completed his assessment, Ted immediately identified the problem *and* the solution! He traced his current unbalanced state back to the first week, when he began to let himself go physically. And almost as quickly, he understood what he needed to adjust to return to being his best—return to a place of strength and balance across all four dimensions. In this case, he knew he needed to focus on the physical. He committed in the coming week to averaging seven hours of sleep each night, getting back on track with his diet, and working out at least three times.

When should you do this trendline assessment? Pausing weekly to assess the arc of your week—when you were up and

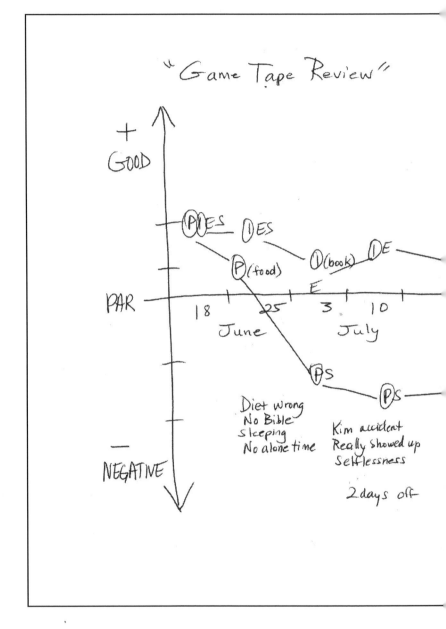

Figure 28. Ted's review and assessment of his previous seven weeks.

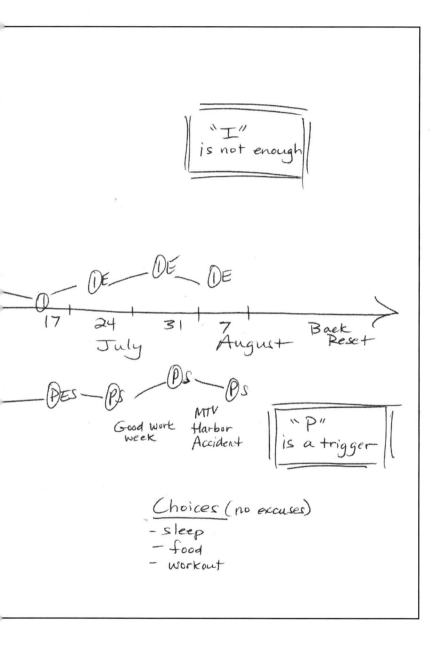

when you were down—would be ideal. Figure out your own rhythm for pausing to self-assess, but do it regularly, even if monthly or quarterly. Remember, the more you notice about yourself, the better opportunity you have to adjust and be your best. This is especially critical during seasons of high stress when you are tempted to default to autopilot.

PERIODIC ASSESSMENT: HOW AM I DOING COMPARED TO MY IDEAL SELF?

 "JOURNAL TIME"

Go to LeadLikeYouBook.com for an exercise related to this assessment.

Before we leave the "how" of assessment, let me offer you one other form of measurement that is available to you with the passage of time and practice.

This version of assessment begins with defining your ideal end in mind—you at your best. You must first know who you aspire to be—the contents of your spiritual dimension. Once you are clear on your identity, your purpose, your beliefs, and your values, then you assess outwardly to see how closely your physical, intellectual, and emotional dimensions align with the spiritual.

Let's go back to a leader I wrote about at the beginning of chapter 6 ("The Spiritual Dimension") to illustrate. If you recall, the first time I met with Brian, regional president for a large financial services company, he confessed to me that he was so tired of feeling ashamed all the time. Though he felt shame as an emotion, it also represented something he felt was missing at his spiritual core—a clear sense of his identity and purpose. Shame says, "I am missing something" or "There is something wrong with me." This message penetrates to our spiritual core.

Part of our work together involved Brian figuring out how he wanted to address this message that shame was sending. Instead of shame defining him, he would define himself—at least who he aspired to be. I encouraged him to work through some of the same exercises I shared with you earlier in chapter 6 under "Spiritual Self-Leadership Challenge 1: Know Who You Are—Identity."

Nine months and a lot of work later, Brian had come a long way in addressing shame and strengthening his spiritual dimension. One of the outcomes was his choice to take his family on a two-week trip to Europe, a vacation he had never allowed himself to consider previously. Before he left, I encouraged him to make some time, while he was disengaged from the routines of work and life, to pause and do some self-reflection to continue to gain clarity on his identity and purpose.

Shortly after his return, he wrote me an email with highlights from his time away. Here is an excerpt from that email:

> My biggest aha of the vacation was as we sat in High Mass at a Church of England in Oxford last Sunday and I had a chance to meditate a little. It hit me that I can boil my IDENTITY down to 5 things. I probably repeated those 5 things to myself 20 times over the last week. They are:
>
> 1) Great husband and father
> 2) Advisor & Encourager
> 3) Prepared
> 4) Refreshed
> 5) With passion!

> I feel really good about these and about how
> they help me be the best me I can be.

Brian has defined his ideal in the five descriptors above. This is who he wants to be. Using these as the standard—Brian at his best—he can then determine how his physical, intellectual, and emotional dimensions need to be aligned with that standard.

His assessment focuses on the difference—how far away he is—from the standard he is holding up for himself. For instance, he can pause and assess "On a scale of 1 to 10, with 10 being best, how am I doing at being a 'great husband and father'? How am I doing as an 'advisor and encourager'?" And so on. This assessment practice reminds him of who he wants to be—his ideal version of himself—and forces him to pause autopilot and be aware of how he is doing relative to that ideal.

This assessment against your ideal self is a good one to use once or twice a year—perhaps during a personal retreat. Try using it *after* you have spent some time with the four dimensions and gained clarity on what that ideal, best version of yourself looks like.

Notice Triggers

Over time, as you get better at pausing, being aware, and assessing, you should begin to see some repeating patterns for when you are at your best and when you are at your "not so best." Ted saw these patterns when he reflected on the seven-week period that led to him being out of whack: laziness in his physical dimension, especially eating poorly, was a trigger that precipitated his downward spiral.

Here are some common triggers I've observed in senior leaders:

- Physical: one too many nights without enough sleep, one too many drinks, nonstop stress leading to chronic sickness or weight gain

- Intellectual: thinking dominated by assumptions rather than facts, obsessive thoughts that crowd out other thinking, nonstop negative thinking about what is going wrong or what could go wrong

- Emotional: allowing certain emotions to build and take over, such as frustration, fear, shame, or sadness

- Spiritual: listening only to external voices while tuning out the "inner voice" of their spiritual core, questioning their self-worth or purpose in life

The point is that we all have triggers unique to us that conspire to keep us from being at our best and from leading with our best. As you get better at assessing, you should also grow more alert to the triggers that take you off your game. Such awareness will help you better avoid those triggers in the first place!

Make Time to Assess

I am not a big fan of annual reviews. I realize this may antagonize my human resource and talent friends. But stay with me. My theory is that HR has to make sure leaders are at least giving annual reviews to compensate for a shortfall that afflicts many in management—failure to give regular everyday feedback to the people they supervise.

Great leaders continually assess and give feedback to those they lead—positive and negative. Those who report to you are entitled to always know where they stand with you. Yes, use an annual review to formalize things for the record, but there should be no anxiety about preparing such a review and no surprises in receiving it—because the assessment and feedback are occurring every day.

In the same way, anytime is a great time to assess yourself using the four dimensions. We said this about being aware in chapter 7. Remember, whenever you assess, you are pausing the autopilot and taking control of who you want to be and how you want to lead.

Here are some times when leaders I work with like to pause, be aware, and assess:

- first thing in the morning, during quiet time or meditation
- on the way to work
- upon first sitting down at their desks
- just before or after a challenging conversation or meeting
- during an afternoon walk around the block
- on the way home from work
- lying in bed just before going to sleep

What about you? How about assessing yourself right now? Turn to the prompts toward the beginning of chapter 7. Pause to be aware. Then assess yourself in each dimension. Finally, give yourself an overall assessment of your readiness to lead.

Not satisfied with where you stand? In the next chapter, we will look at how you can adjust to get closer to where you want to be.

KEY TAKEAWAYS

- Assessment is a necessary next step following awareness. It brings measurement and focus to more accurately identify the gap between how I'm doing right now and how I can be when I'm at my best.

- I am the best judge of who I am when I'm at my best.

- I can choose whatever scale I want for assessment (1 to 100 percent; 1 to 10; or A,B, C, D, and F). With repetition, my scale will become more meaningful to me.

- Like being aware, anytime is a good time to pause and assess.

- I can assess myself in a variety of ways:

    - Basic assessment—how am I doing right now?

    - Trendline assessment—how am I doing over time?

- Periodic assessment—how am I doing compared to my ideal self?

- When I assess routinely, I should begin to see helpful patterns as well as triggers that knock me off my game, preventing me from leading well.

QUESTIONS FOR REFLECTION

- What is the difference between noticing (awareness) and assigning a value to all you are noticing (assessment)? How can assessing help you lead better?

- What scale would you like to use regularly to assess how you are doing in your four dimensions?

- What are some words or phrases you would use to describe you "at your best" in each of the four dimensions?

- What are some good times in your day or week to routinely pause and assess how you are doing?

- What are one or more triggers you have (and in which dimensions) that can lead you away from being your best?

- **Go to LeadLikeYouBook.com for additional exercises related to this chapter.**

CHAPTER 10

ADJUST

Everyone thinks of changing the world, but no one thinks of changing himself.
—Leo Tolstoy

Being a person is a challenge, but I think I'm a better one than I used to be.
—Tom Petty

When I got on the phone with Mike for our coaching session, he barely let me say hello.

"Rob, we've got issues!" I soon realized Mike was sharing *his* issues with *me*, which to him now made them *our* issues!

He continued: "Last week, I had trouble breathing. I couldn't sleep at night because of my breathing. I went to see my doctor, who ran an EKG and a bunch of tests. He told me that, medically, I'm fine. But my job is killing me."

It turns out Mike was suffering from something very real: anxiety hyperventilation. He was taking short, rapid breaths constantly. As a result, his body was getting *too much* oxygen.

His doctor told him it was all stress related, and his prescription was for Mike to make some adjustments to address the stress.

Indeed, Mike had lots of sources of stress at the time he went to see his doctor. During the previous three weeks, he had been finalizing a $400 million acquisition, closing an East Coast office, letting half of the employees go and relocating the balance to California, and revamping his company's product line—all of which added up to a perfect storm of anxiety-producing stressors.

I asked him how he assessed his overall readiness to lead at that moment on a scale of 1 to 10. His answer: 4.

Because we had been through this exercise many times before (though never with so much stress that had him hyperventilating!), Mike knew how to evaluate himself in each of the four dimensions.

"I'm at a 4 physically. I feel tense and tired. Intellectually, I give myself a 5—my head is just a jumble of thoughts, and I'm not thinking clearly. Emotionally, I feel fear. I'm afraid I won't lead well through all this transition. And I'm angry that I can't think straight! I give myself a 3 emotionally. And in the spiritual dimension . . . Wow! That's a 2. I'm totally disconnected from feeling grounded, connected to my purpose, and confident in my identity as a leader."

Mike's opening statement—"we've got issues"—really meant "Something has got to change. I need to make some adjustments." He was self-aware. And he had assessed. Now he knew he needed to adjust so he could lead with more than just a 4.

IS THIS CHAPTER NECESSARY?

I have discovered two interesting phenomena over my years of coaching senior leaders, representing their two areas of greatest need when it comes to personal growth.

The first is that leaders most need help with self-awareness. For years, they have been learning so much about what I will call "the world outside themselves." They've learned essential skills required for their jobs, what it takes to compete in the marketplace or industries they work in, and how to interact with and influence others as leaders. School has taught them the basic skills; on-the-job experience has taught them about their industry; and management training programs, observing others, seminars, and reading have taught them leadership skills.

But the topic they often know least about is "the world *inside* themselves." This is why I spend so much time up front helping them get to know themselves better through self-awareness. And it is why nearly two-thirds of this book is devoted to awareness.

What happens when the smart leaders I work with gain vastly improved self-awareness? Once they see, and assess, they often *know* what they need to do to adjust. This is consistent with all that has gotten them into their leadership positions in the first place—when they clearly understand the problem, the challenge, or the situation, they *know* what needs adjusting. Therefore I ask the question, "Is this chapter really necessary?" Read on to see why I believe it is.

One day, I ran into the president of a company where I have been coaching the CEO for the last five months. A colleague of mine is coaching the president and three other senior executives of this company. The president said to me, "You need to know that we are already seeing a big change in David [their CEO]. He is more open to feedback than ever. He does less bulldozing through people when they throw out objections or slow him down. As a result, more of us are willing to give him feedback than previously. We sure hope this can continue."

This CEO is changing, and those around him can see it. Guess what? I didn't teach this CEO to be less obstinate and more open. I never told him he needed to talk less and listen more. I, as his coach, never dangled the prospect that his people would trust him more and be more honest with him. He figured out how to adjust on his own, after becoming more aware and better at assessing.

So I wrote this chapter with the assumption that many of the adjustments you need to make will be self-evident. You will know what you need to do to adjust. It would take another book altogether (and these books already exist[38]) to catalog all the adjustments different leaders need to make to be more effective. What follows in this chapter are some basic go-to moves that will be helpful every day.

> Knowing what to adjust is not enough. . . .
> You have to actually make the adjustment.

But knowing what to adjust by itself does not result in personal growth or change. And this leads me to the second great need I have observed with high-performing leaders: you have to actually *make* the adjustment.

You have to do it! Do you remember this example from chapter 8? I can be aware that I currently weigh 215 pounds. I can assess that I would be healthier if I weighed 195 pounds. And I can know that I need to adjust by losing twenty pounds. But nothing changes until I make the adjustment and lose the weight.

Adjustments can be quick, momentary shifts or longer-term, transformational shifts that require us to keep adjusting over days, weeks, or months.

I remind leaders that real, lasting change occurs in degrees—very gradually. A change in my weight will occur only with daily adjustments in my eating and exercise. And even after I make it to 195 pounds or less, I will need to continue to adjust for the change to last. Repeated short-term adjustments become long-term adjustments—which become lasting change.

OUR ADJUSTMENT GOAL: STRENGTH AND BALANCE

Let's return to the story at the beginning of this chapter. In the situation Mike finds himself in, it is obvious he wants to be leading with more than a 4. His company *needs* him to be leading with more than a 4. How does Mike, and how do you, adjust accordingly, using the four dimensions?

You will be the best version of yourself, and more ready to lead, if you aim for *strength* and *balance* across all four dimensions. In other words, it is not enough to make an adjustment in just one dimension and consider the job done.

Remember our discussion of your default dimension in chapter 8? Depending on whether you default to your head, your heart, or your body, especially when feeling pressure or stress, you may feel it is sufficient for your dominant dimension to be in good shape while the other three dimensions are running on fumes.

Mike may believe that simply a good night's sleep (physical) will be enough to help him get back on track. He'll just "gut" it out. Getting some sleep will help him some, and he may move the dial slightly from a 4 to a 5, but Mike is short-changing himself if he doesn't work on adjustments in the other three dimensions at the same time—dealing with his emotions, getting more focused intellectually, and connecting more with his purpose and identity spiritually. Strength in each dimension, and then balance across all four, is the target for adjustment (figure 29).

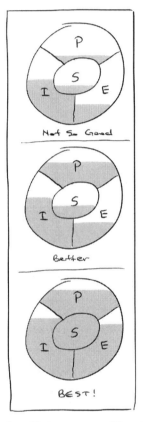

Figure 29. Adjust for strength and balance across all four dimensions.

There are two types of adjustments you can make to move toward being your best: short term and long term. Short-term adjustments are immediately helpful but short in duration (seconds, minutes, or hours). However, when repeated, they become helpful building blocks to making long-term adjustments. You can do short-term adjustments on the fly and undercover—no one has to even know you're using them.

Long-term adjustments, on the other hand, are a big deal! Because they represent major change, they will likely take months or even years to accomplish.[39] And they will be transformational—you will fundamentally change as a leader. Long-term adjustments are difficult (if they were easy, you would have already made them!). Making the change requires dogged determination on your part, preferably with the encouragement of a few close friends.

Short-Term Adjustments

Short-term adjustments are ones that you can make right now, and you will immediately be in a different position to lead better. I sometimes call them tactical adjustments, because, just as soldiers adapt to changing circumstances in combat, you make them on the fly as needed. Be aware, assess, and adjust (figure 30). You make the adjustment to help you in the next minute, or in the next twenty-four hours. And no one has to know; this is agile self-leadership: adjusting as the situation dictates.

Short-term, tactical adjustments:

- can be done anytime
- can be done in the next minute or the next twenty-four hours
- are internal—no one needs to know
- yield temporary benefits
- can become habitual and transformative, when they are done long enough

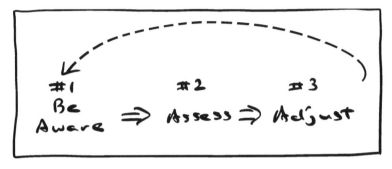

Figure 30. Be aware, assess, and adjust. Repeat.

What are some examples of short-term adjustments? As I said earlier, I believe a lot of the time that the best adjustment will be self-evident to you. If you have paused the autopilot long enough to be aware, and then to assess, you will likely know what you need to do next to adjust and improve your readiness to lead.

This was the case with Mike. About fifteen minutes into our call, after I asked him to turn off autopilot and notice himself in four dimensions, he told me he could immediately feel his stress decreasing. He was suddenly less anxious emotionally. Physically, he noticed the tightness in his chest easing, and he was more relaxed in his body in general. Notice that with these two simple adjustments—turning off autopilot and noticing—in a fifteen-minute span, Mike was already in a better place. This adjustment then opened up the possibility in our coaching call for him to consider some longer-term adjustments to reduce the chance of him having to see his doctor for hyperventilation anxiety again (and indeed, he hasn't!).

Below are a number of what I call "go-to" moves— short-term adjustments you can use anytime and in a variety of situations. Try one or two of them right now. I'm guessing you are in a relatively peaceful, comfortable, secure place as you read this book. To best understand how to apply these, think back to a day or an incident from the past week when you were aware of not being at your best—you were stressed, angry, afraid, whatever. You wish you could have a do-over. Pause right now for a couple of minutes—be aware in all four dimensions, then assess your readiness to lead, or perhaps just your readiness to be present. Then try one of these adjustments.

Breathe one to two breaths. Breathe in slowly, taking fresh oxygen all the way down deep into your lungs. Count to five or ten on each inhale and exhale. This is one of the most fundamental adjustments you can make to disengage your autopilot. Instead of impulsively reacting in the moment, you create a momentary pause for a thoughtful response. It buys you time if you are in a tense conversation. Oh, and you just fed some fresh oxygen into your bloodstream, enabling your body to release a little tension and your brain to think more clearly.

Breathe for one or two minutes. Sit quietly and breathe slowly, as in the adjustment above, but for an extended period. Follow the breath into your body, down your airway, and down further into your lungs. Keep following your breath downward, downward toward your gut (with practice, this downward focus draws your attention away from the distracting thoughts and feelings in your head and heart). This breathing exercise can be a preparatory adjustment used prior to some of the others in this list. It could be something you do as a matter of routine, at certain times each day, or impromptu as needed. One to two minutes could seem like a lifetime if you are used to nonstop, frenetic activity. Stay with it anyway, and begin to experience the benefits!

Focus on the present. Let go of thoughts or feelings about what just happened or what is next, and come into the right now. Get out of past tense or future tense, and come into the present tense. "Be" in your body, "be" in the room, "be" present to others, or "be" present to yourself if there are no others. This practice can help take the edge off the past (sadness, resentment, or disappointment) as well as the future (fears, concerns, or time pressure). Focus on what is right in front of you. Only by being present to something can you do anything about it.

Focus on gratitude. No matter how stressful things get, you still have plenty for which you can be thankful.[40] Start counting the good things in your life. As a leader, much of your job is spent identifying and solving problems. This tendency can lead to a habitually negative and critical mindset, frustration at all that is wrong, and criticism of yourself and others. Counterbalance it with gratitude for what is good, for what you have, and for what is going well. To paraphrase a Jewish proverb, "A grateful heart is good medicine!"[41]

> Only by being present to something
> can you do anything about it.

Get moving. For those of us who can be overwhelmed by our thoughts (including me!) or our emotions at times, sometimes the best adjustment is to get up out of your seat, walk out of your office, and go somewhere. Once I was with a chief marketing officer in New York City, who sat before me paralyzed with emotional stress following some negative feedback from his boss. He could hardly talk. At my urging, he finally stood up, walked out of the office, took the elevator down to the street, and walked a few blocks around Lower Manhattan. When he returned, he was a different man.

When we move, we engage the physical dimension of our bodies, which gives a little less energy to the intellectual and emotional dimensions. When we move, our perspective shifts, we see things from a different angle, and we feel differently.

Talk it out. Sitting and trying to contain our impulses, thoughts, or emotions can sometimes feel like a pressure cooker heating up. We feel we might explode—generally in a way that would not represent good leadership! An immediate adjustment is to find someone and talk with them. How many times have I heard these statements from leaders: "I just feel better being able to talk it out" or "It helps me to simply think out loud"? And often, we didn't even solve their problems! They have merely been able to open up a bit and relieve some of the pressure. My wife, Marta, serves in this role for me every day. You should have one or two people in your inner circle with whom you can talk things out.

Write it out. This is an alternative to talking it out. And it is always available to you. Get the swirl of thoughts, emotions, or agitations down on paper: "Right now I am thinking . . ." (intellectual) or "Right now I am bothered by feelings of . . ." (emotional) or "Right now I feel like . . . [some sort of bad behavior] (physical)." Then read your words. This crucial step is *conscious noticing* (instead of autopilot) and helps you deliberately adjust instead of being stuck with unacknowledged and negative forces at work within you. Once you've written it out and acknowledged what is going on, consider taking the next step by completing this sentence: "Instead, I would like to focus my thoughts/feelings/energy toward. . . ." Identify the adjustment you want to make in that moment.

Think different. Apple developed an ad campaign around these two words in the late 1990s—for good reason. Steve Jobs wanted to shake up people's perspective on computing. That couldn't happen with the same old thinking. Whether you want to admit it or not, you can get into a rut with *how* you are thinking—the logic you apply to problems and decisions.

One common rut is thinking that others should be thinking about things the same way you are. If only they saw your logic, they would agree with you! The more you dig into your way of thinking, the deeper that rut gets, until it traps you into believing there is only one way to think—your way. Another wise Proverb helps here: "As a person thinketh, so are they."[42] The way you think dictates your behavior. And your behavior dictates results. In reverse, if you want different results, you need different behavior, which requires different thinking. I keep a little card on my desk with the question "What would you do if you knew nothing could stop you?" One of the best ways to start thinking differently and open up possibilities is to ask, "What if . . . ?"

Change up your schedule. Maintaining the same schedule day in and day out is a great way to stay on autopilot. You go mindlessly from one meeting to the next, a slave to the routine of your schedule. More than once I have been alongside leaders who are in really tough spots, yet they feel helpless to pause and adjust because their schedules tell them they need to get to the next thing. You may need to simply carve out thirty minutes so you can take a refreshing walk outside. Or maybe you begin tomorrow morning on your back porch or at a quiet coffee shop instead of going straight to the office. Figure out your best times for thinking and your best times for interacting with others, and as much as you can, adjust your schedule accordingly.

Shift to a different dimension. When the current dimension you are operating from has you stuck or when you recognize one dimension is in overload, consciously shift to a different dimension. Sometimes, as I think about what to write, I have trouble sorting out my thoughts. To remedy this, I often shift to my physical dimension by mixing in some exercise or moving to a different location. Salespeople know to stand up (physical) to help overcome their fear (emotional) of making a cold call. Logic (intellectual) can be a great counterbalance when you are overly emotional about a topic. Any intentional adjustment to a different dimension is a movement toward strength and balance across all four dimensions.

Reconnect with your purpose. This is what I call a "master move" in shifting to a different dimension. For me, when I am off balance, worried, or worn out, it is so helpful to have this inner dialogue with myself: "Wait a minute. Who am I and why am I here?" Reminding myself that I am a leadership coach and am here to help leaders be better versions of themselves is very grounding for me. Intentionally moving to your spiritual dimension by pausing to reconnect with your identity and purpose can ease physical tension, wound-up emotions, or unhelpful thoughts.

Finally, let me encourage you with lessons about short-term adjustments that I have learned from coaching leaders.

Short-term adjustments will often be self-evident. Don't feel that you need to reference this book or a checklist for every move. If you are self-disciplined enough to pause and be aware, you are halfway there! Assess and then make a creative adjustment that will help you shift toward strength in a particular dimension and balance across all four dimensions.

Short-term adjustments may feel awkward. At first, making the adjustment will feel awkward. You're not used to doing it. You are in the comfortable habit of being on autopilot. As you adjust, you may be highly self-conscious of your performance, as if everyone else is watching (generally they are not!). Stay with it. After a while, you will be so comfortable with the adjustment that you will fine-tune it to be even more useful.

Short-term adjustments can become long-term habits. Over time, an adjustment that originally seemed awkward can become automatic. With practice, you routinely take deeper breaths, relax tension in your shoulders, smile, think positive thoughts, or contemplate gratitude. These strengthening habits help build the bridge toward your longer-term transformation.

One or more short-term adjustments would have helped
you with the do-over scenario you thought of earlier. With
time, and consciously turning off the autopilot, you will
develop other go-to moves of your own to be a better version
of yourself on a moment's notice.

Long-Term Adjustments

What do we mean by long-term adjustments? These are more
than mere momentary impulses to change or improve. These
adjustments are intended to really move the needle on your
leadership effectiveness—to help you transform! Here are some
examples of transformational goals representing long-term
adjustments that my clients have worked on over the years:

- "I will be more proactive and less reactive with
  people and situations. I will spend more time
  pursuing established goals and vision than 'being
  a firefighter.'"

- "I am committed to directing and leading others
  more to get work done versus doing all the work
  myself. I will get out of the weeds so that I can
  lead better."

- "I will regularly give positive and meaningful
  feedback to my team."

- "I will act with more courage and self-confidence.
  I will trust my instincts, especially in my interactions with the executive team."

- "I will improve my strategic-planning capabilities and contribute more to the company's strategic initiatives."

- "I will be a leader who holds my people accountable for their performance."

> **Long-term, transformational adjustments:**
>
> - have a clear goal
> - are grounded in purpose
> - can be reached with the help of trusted friends
> - are repeated over a long time to create a habit
> - can feel like taking "two steps forward, one step back"

By the way, all the examples above came from the C-suite—CEOs, COOs, CFOs, and presidents—leaders who already have significant capabilities but have identified at least one adjustment they need to make if they (and those they lead) are to move forward. They have relied on their many other talents to get them to this point but have assessed themselves and confronted the reality that "what got me here won't get me there!" These are smart, accomplished leaders who know how they need to adjust but recognize it will take practice and repetition to make the adjustment a habit.

In each of the examples above, the goal represents a significant transformation for these leaders. They may have known for many years that they needed to change, or perhaps it has just become clear to them in the last couple of months working with me as their coach. Either way, knowing what needs to change and actually making the change are two different things. Remember, change begins with self-awareness, but self-awareness does not equal change.

> Change begins with self-awareness, but
> self-awareness does not equal change.

Back to Mike briefly. He ended up developing a long-term adjustment game plan so that he could "worry less about what others think of me and lead more from within—lead with self-confidence." One of the big contributors to his extreme stress had been his anxiety over what some employees thought about his push to revamp their product line. He realized that as a leader he needed to get their input, but at the end of the day, he needed to make the tough decision and see it through. This choice took intentional work because it addressed the shadow side of Mike's strength: Mike was a popular leader with his employees, but sometimes he was susceptible to self-doubt when his leadership decisions were not universally popular.

Here is the Personal Action Plan Mike wrote to pursue his goal.

My development goal. *How do I need to improve or change?*

I will worry less about what others think of me and lead more from within—lead with self-confidence.

My purpose. *For the sake of "what" am I doing this? How will I and my organization benefit?*

I must make this change to be less of a reactive leader. Instead, I will be able to lead with more of my own creativity and intention. My company will benefit by having a leader who moves more quickly instead of being wishy-washy or delaying to get consensus. Also, I am leading this company because I have years of accumulated experience and wisdom that needs to be expressed in my leadership.

My new behaviors. *What are tangible ways I, and others, will know I have improved or changed?*

- I will pause and ask myself, "What do I think?"

- When I am ready, I will say out loud, "I think we should. . . ."

- On tough decisions, I will make a T diagram, listing out what others think and what I think.

- I will make decisions more quickly and stand by those decisions instead of changing course if I get some opposition.

- To be better at connecting with my inner wisdom, I will pause and do a self-awareness exercise for fifteen minutes at the beginning of every workday.

- When I am wrestling with self-doubt or low self-confidence over an issue, I will discuss it within twenty-four hours with my wife or my coach instead of letting it fester inside me.

My trade-offs: *What will I need to give up?*
I will let go of making everyone happy about every decision.
My obstacles: *What obstacles or difficulties may exist? How will I manage them?*

My obstacle is that I may revert back to old ways if someone doesn't like my decision. In response, I will say to myself, "I have considered everyone's input, including this person's, and, along with my wisdom and experience, I have decided. . . . Now it is time to move on."

My stakeholders: *Who should know what I am doing, and can support me, as I pursue this goal?*

Stakeholder	Specific Request of Stakeholder
Colleen (wife)	Ask me periodically if I am wrestling with self-doubt or low self-confidence; be a talking partner.
Joe (peer)	Observe me; when I fall back into old patterns, call me out. When you see me acting with greater self-confidence, listening to my own voice as well as others, tell me.
Rob (coach)	Hold me accountable by reviewing checklist of New Behaviors regularly.

My resources: *What resources do I need (i.e., reading, training, exercises, etc.)?*

I will read the book *Extreme Ownership*.[43]

So how do you tackle your own transformational adjustment toward being a better leader? Here are proven steps that I use with leaders like Mike every day in the form of a Personal Action Plan. For each step, you can reference Mike's action plan above. A blank template can be found at the end of this chapter (see figure 31) and at LeadLikeYouBook.com.

1. Write down your goal. When you set a really significant organizational goal, what do you do? You write it down. It's something you will be pursuing for months, maybe even years. So you clearly articulate the goal and "memorialize it" by writing it down, so you and those who will be helping you (see item 5 below) can reference it over time.

2. Anchor your goal in purpose. Getting clear on the compelling purpose for pursuing your change goal is essential to sticking with it. This isn't just a goal that would be *nice* to achieve; it is *necessary* to achieve. Losing weight to simply look good is a nice reason. Losing weight to avoid early onset diabetes or heart problems represents a necessary purpose. So as you consider your goal, ask these questions to clarify what is at stake: "How will I or my organization benefit if I succeed? What are the consequences if I fail?"

3. Describe the "new you." In what tangible ways will you, and those around you, know you have changed? The emphasis here is on the word "tangible." This means behavioral change—people seeing with their eyes and hearing with their ears a new version of you. It is not enough for you to simply *think* differently or *feel* differently (though both of those will be important). You have to *behave* differently. After all, it's only through behaving and talking in new ways that we get new results. Write out a checklist of new behaviors you will be able to hold yourself accountable to—you are either doing these things (and making the long-term adjustment), or you are not. Progress will be black and white. Make this list as long as you can. A nice target is eight to ten items that exemplify the change you want to see in yourself.

4. Identify and plan for your biggest obstacles. What one or two old habits are most likely to get in the way of making the long-term adjustment you need to make? These are your obstacles. They *will* come up. They *will* try to force you back to your old ways of behaving. And you need to have a game plan for when they present themselves. The best defense is a good offense. You want to be proactively ready with a plan to act differently, rather than stay on autopilot and go back to the nonresourceful ways you responded in the past.

5. Enlist the support of stakeholders. Rule number one of real, lasting change is to let others know what you aspire to do and ask for their help. This requires a bit of humility, and it means asking people you can trust. You are asking them for two things in particular: encouragement ("When you see me behaving in these new ways, will you tell me and encourage me to keep doing them?") and constructive feedback ("When you see me falling back into old patterns, will you give me that feedback and encourage me back toward my change goal?"). This is where having a personal leadership coach can be so helpful—someone who is pulling for you, pushing you, and helping you do the hard work of adjusting toward a better version of yourself.

6. Review regularly. You have a well-written plan, clear objectives, and friends and family supporting you. The final step (or steps) is to review your plan on a regular basis and hold yourself accountable for making progress. Keep reviewing and engaging with your plan until you, along with your stakeholders, believe you have transformed this aspect of your leadership.

Set whatever schedule will help you keep your goal at the top of your mind. Perhaps your frequency could be the following schedule:

- Daily, for the first two weeks, read over the plan until it is memorized.
- Weekly, for the first four weeks, discuss progress and challenges with your stakeholders.
- Monthly, during months two through six,[44] continue to discuss progress and challenges with your stakeholders.

KEYS TO SUCCESSFUL LONG-TERM ADJUSTMENT

Years of helping leaders successfully make long-term adjustments have taught me a few things. Keep these in mind as you embark on your own transformation.

Prioritize and take one thing at a time. Success-oriented leaders like to identify *everything* that needs fixing and then tackle it all. They apply this tendency to fixing themselves as well. I force them to pick just one thing for long-term adjustment (okay, I let a few insistent types take on two things!). The reason is that we are talking *big change*! If you succeed, the payoffs should be big. Because you have limited bandwidth for self-development, you need to focus all of that attention on this one area. Make progress one goal at a time. Once you succeed, then move on to the next transformational adjustment.

> Progress, not perfection, is the goal
> with long-term adjustments.

Be patient with yourself. You didn't get this way overnight, so don't expect to change immediately either. In fact, don't be surprised if your work feels like two steps forward and one step back. And don't measure progress from one day to the next. For proper perspective, I will often ask my leaders, "How are you doing in this area today versus nine to twelve months ago?" That perspective helps them realize they are actually making progress.

Beware your hazardous environment! You are enthusiastic and ambitious regarding your personal transformation. But guess what? Everyone around you (except your stakeholders who know about your plan) is expecting the same old you to keep showing up. They have actually gotten quite used to the old you, and because they are comfortable with the old you, they could be the ones who present some of the biggest barriers to your personal growth.

Your goal is to delegate more; their goal is for you to keep doing all the work. Your goal is to better hold people accountable; their goal is to not be accountable. Your goal is to ask powerful questions; their goal is for you to keep giving them all the answers. Just as it will take you a while to change, it will take those around you a while to realize you really are changing! Don't let your environment push you back to your old ways of doing things.

Embrace the discomfort. I remind my leaders that the magnitude of their discomfort in making a change mirrors the magnitude of the change itself. In other words, if your long-term adjustment goal is not very big, it probably won't feel very risky, scary, or uncomfortable. Human nature is to stay in our comfort zone. Autopilot keeps us in our comfort zone. But if you are ambitious, and you want to pursue change that is really going to move the needle on your leadership effectiveness, it is inevitably going to feel awkward for you at first. So embrace the discomfort—it's actually a sign your adjustment is significant!

* * *

A while ago, I found myself suffering along with fellow passengers on a chronically delayed flight late at night, waiting to depart Dulles Airport outside Washington, DC. As we sat in the terminal after deplaning for the second time and hoping to board again, I couldn't help but notice a young woman in the waiting area who was on the same flight.

She was extremely angry, talking loudly into her phone and complaining to the person on the other end. She talked nonstop, and literally every fourth word out of her mouth was an F-bomb.

Her loud voice, laced with profanity, bothered me so much that I got up and moved away from her to the other side of the waiting area. But even after I moved, she continued to distract me. I was getting angry at her being so angry! As someone who travels frequently and experiences occasional travel problems, I began forming my own story about this stranger, judging her and looking down on her for not exercising more self-control. And my anger distracted me from doing anything productive as I waited.

But then something happened! Turning off *autopilot*, I had a little conversation with myself. "Rob! Notice how you're behaving [*awareness*]! You're a coach! And you coach leaders in handling situations like this all the time. You can do better here [*assessment*]!"

I decided to suspend my judgments and explanations of the woman's behavior and instead get curious. I moved back to sit closer to her, and I waited until she finished her phone call. Eventually I caught her eyes and said simply, "Rough day, huh [*adjustment!*]?"

My curiosity opened up a dialogue. I learned that she lived in Miami. Her mom lived in Queens. And the day before, she had received some really bad news. A biopsy had come back. Her mother had cancer and needed an operation as soon as possible. This young woman, who didn't travel a lot, had scrambled to arrange a flight to be with her mom immediately. She had been traveling all day and had had complications with other flights. And now, as we sat there, having gotten on and off this flight twice, she was nearly at her wits' end. She was frightened, angry, and alone.

I wish I could tell you I had something particularly profound to say to her, something that made everything better. But about all I could do was communicate to her that I cared and that I was sorry all of this was happening to her. After a couple of minutes of her talking and me sympathizing—us connecting—she began to visibly calm down. Perhaps my changing who I was in the moment helped her change.

We eventually boarded the plane and took off. As I reflected, I realized I had received another lesson in how I need to, and can, keep getting better.

I'm not perfect, and I never will be. But I'm getting better. I'm being more of who I was meant to be. And I hope by now you see concrete steps for how you can get better and lead like you were meant to.

Focus your attention on the person over whom you have 100 percent control—you!

- Pause and turn off your **autopilot**.
- Turn on **awareness—physically, intellectually, emotionally, and spiritually.**
- **Assess** how you're doing overall.
- Make the **adjustment** you need to make.

That's how a leader gets better!

Now turn the page to one last chapter, and read the stories of three good leaders who got even better.

My Development Goal -- *How do I need to improve or change?*

My Purpose -- *For the sake of "what" am I doing this? How will I and/or my organization benefit?*

My Expected Outcomes -- *What are tangible ways I, and others, will know I have improved or changed?*

My Trade-offs -- *What will I need to give up?*

My Obstacles -- *What obstacles or difficulties may exist? How will I manage them?*

Obstacle: Response:

My Stakeholders -- *Who should know what I am doing, and can support me, as I pursue this goal?*

Stakeholder(s):   Specific Request of stakeholder(s):

My Resources -- *What resources do I need? i.e. reading, training, exercises, etc.?*

Figure 31. My Personal Action Plan, a solid plan for long-term adjustments.

KEY TAKEAWAYS

- After turning off autopilot, turning on awareness in four dimensions, and assessing, the last necessary step is adjusting—changing.

- Most of the time, the adjustments I need to make are obvious. The real challenge comes in actually making the adjustment—changing! Change begins with self-awareness, but self-awareness alone is not change.

- Two types of adjustments are available to me:

    - short-term: quick shifts in the moment

    - long-term: lead to transformational change

- The goal of adjustment is to increase strength and balance across all four of my dimensions.

- A written plan with a clearly stated goal and purpose is a critical tool for longer-term transformation. Reviewing the plan regularly and having at least one other person to help hold me accountable will help me make the change.

- I need to remember that real change is difficult and takes time. I didn't become who I am overnight. Changing into who I want to be requires patience with myself.

- I now have the tools to become a better version of myself every day—to lead like I was meant to!

QUESTIONS FOR REFLECTION

- As you have learned to turn off autopilot, be aware, and assess, what are some obvious adjustments you have already identified or made in yourself?

- Think of one or two areas where you have made a big, positive change in yourself in the past. What were the factors that helped you be successful at making the change?

- From the short-term adjustments referenced in chapter 10, or your own list, what are one or two go-to moves you want to remember for adjusting in the future?

- What are one or two long-term adjustments you would like to make to be a better version of yourself in the future? What would be so good about you making this change? When would you like to start? Who do you want to tell?

- **Go to LeadLikeYouBook.com for additional exercises related to this chapter.**

CHAPTER 11

THREE LEADERS WHO GOT BETTER

I hope, over the time you have been reading this book, you have actually begun to experience change in yourself, and you see the opportunity for even more transformative growth.

So before closing, let me share with you the true stories of three leaders who got better by following this process. They are merely a sampling of all the leaders in whom my fellow coaches and I have witnessed change. While your goal for change will be different from theirs, you can still see how the process has worked in the lives of real leaders like you.

I have italicized key terms discussed in the first ten chapters so that you can see how they weave together to form a tapestry of transformation that helped these leaders lead like they were meant to.

HELEN, THE PERFECTIONIST

Even though we had never met before, when I first sat down with Helen at our kickoff coaching session, I felt like I already knew her. This was because I had been hearing about her for the previous six months as I coached one of her peers. Helen was his one colleague who always irritated him. And to hear him describe her, she irritated everyone else too.

The reality was Helen fixed things others had screwed up! And she did it really well. Her reward for doing so was a promotion so she could have greater influence, and get more things fixed, across the platform of her whole company. Her challenge was that, in her pursuit of excellence, she left people in her wake; she was oblivious to how she was alienating them. She needed to get better as a leader to make this transition. And I got to be her coach.

When they were asked, "What new skills or behaviors would make this leader more effective?" here are the comments Helen's two bosses made as she began her coaching:

- **Boss A.** Balancing her strong technical skills and drive for outcomes with attention to encouraging the heart of all her colleagues will enable her to have an even greater impact on the organization and its individuals.

- **Boss B.** Helen does an excellent job "reading the room" but often is impatient with the progress of others. While her goal-driven agenda is incredibly important, if she is to gain the support of others, it is important that she "lead at a pace they can follow."

What jumps out to you in their feedback? Do you notice the *great strength* of her "goal-driven agenda" and "drive for outcomes" has a corresponding *great weakness*: a shadow side that is impatient, discourages others, and risks alienation? Helen didn't see it until she paused to notice. And then she noticed more.

As Helen described herself for the first time, even before we gathered feedback from her bosses and others, these phrases jumped out at me:

- "I'm a perfectionist."
- "I'm hyperfocused around goals."
- "I defer to the negative."
- "I desire to control."
- "I have a fear of failure."
- "'I work hard' is one of my guiding principles."

Think about how these self-perceptions found their way into her *autopilot* ways of showing up in all *four* of her *dimensions*. Helen thought all that mattered were her results: getting things fixed perfectly for her company. But she failed to see there were other not-so-good results: turning off and discouraging the very people she was supposed to be leading. She could improve and perfect things as an individual. But she would fail to gain leverage as a leader and make even more improvements through her team.

As I invited Helen to pause and reflect, she began to see the roots of identity, purpose, beliefs, and values in her *spiritual* dimension. She had grown up with an alcoholic and abusive father whose harsh words rang in her little-girl ears: "Without me you are nothing!" What does a child do in response to that message? Little Helen chose this mantra: "I will never be dependent on someone else. And I will stay out of trouble by working hard and always being good."

This mantra permeated outward from her spiritual dimension into the thoughts, feelings, and behaviors of her other three dimensions. As I had her review incidents from work she wished she could do over, she began to notice that anger was ever present in her *emotional* dimension, and she identified her *spiritual* identity as "The Fixer." As weeks passed, she realized that, in addition to being angry and judgmental with her subordinates and peers, she was first of all angry and judgmental with *herself*!

Finally, she homed in on perfection as a primary *autopilot* mode. Everything needed to be perfect. Everyone needed to be perfect. She needed to be perfect. With growing *self-awareness*, she could finally *assess*: "I'm never going to be that perfect person." Now she could begin to *adjust* how she was leading—both herself and others.

In writing her Personal Action Plan, Helen's goal became "to broaden my collaboration and consensus-building skills with internal and external colleagues so as to improve our team's development and transformation." Notice the goal was to "improve," not to "perfect"!

To put this goal into action, she listed the following behaviors she would practice.

When engaging with others I will:

- begin each meeting with a smile and appreciate those present
- pause to inquire about others' personal lives and what is important to them outside of work
- seek to understand others' purpose and what they want to accomplish in their work
- allow others to speak first and seek opinions of the team fully
- allow and embrace appropriate silence within meetings and one-on-one time

When receiving feedback from colleagues, I will:

- welcome and appreciate input and feedback
- listen and thank the person for the insight and perspective

- genuinely acknowledge the value when feedback is given

Helen put these new practices into action. As she redirected her perfectionist tendencies into her action plan goal, she gradually became a better leader. She was leading others better because she was leading herself better from within. Without compromising her results, she stopped being so hard on herself and demanding perfection 100 percent of the time. As a result, she was more at peace with herself and more collaborative with those around her.

Before our coaching concluded, she received a significant raise, a tangible vote of confidence from her bosses that she was on the right path to leading in new ways. And, interestingly, she asked me to facilitate a meeting between herself and the previous leader whom she irritated so much. When the meeting was over, they were both able to laugh at themselves and agreed to encourage one another as the new leader each was striving to be.

EVAN, THE PEOPLE PLEASER

Evan was being groomed to run a major new division of his company. He had proven how valuable he was in other parts of the company, building a reputation as a leader who got things done, and his CEO wanted him to spearhead a new business. But the CEO had some lingering concerns about Evan's leadership that he wanted Evan to address through coaching.

When I sat with Evan and his boss, his boss said, "Evan needs to be more *self-aware*. He keeps things to himself; then we find out later there is a problem. I tell him to do something; he will nod, but then he will go and do what he wants to do. And if the results are not good, he will blame others." He summarized: "Evan needs to stop trying to be a one-man army and instead consider the views of others and include them in the work."

Later, as I met alone with him and began asking questions to open up our coaching, Evan said, "I think I'm very successful at making people think I'm okay and happy." Consider what Evan might look like on *autopilot* as he puts up this appearance. One thing he noticed early on: "I smile all the time."

In the opening briefing with his boss, and later just the two of us, we started to see the outline of Evan's *great strength* and his *great weakness*. In his efforts to put up a good appearance that he is on top of everything, he can be deceptive and cover up problems. His boss and others are not always sure they can trust Evan.

As he began to learn about and practice *self-awareness*, Evan had a difficult conversation one day with his boss. I asked him to replay the incident, noticing what was happening in him through the *four-dimensional* lens. Here are his highlights:

- Physical: "I felt like moving away from [his boss]; I had that feeling in my torso, as if my body was preparing for pain."

- Intellectual: "I remember feeling stupid. I had all these conflicting thoughts in my head that kept me from having a clear answer for him."

- Emotional: "Shame. Like I was telling myself, 'You need to be better than this.'"

- Spiritual: "I want [my boss] to respect me, to believe in me, to know that I am on top of things."

As he reflected on all the points of self-awareness in this difficult conversation, Evan realized how much he was on *autopilot*—not quite knowing what to tell his boss but still wanting to appear like he had it all together. He said, "There is a pattern for me in these sorts of encounters to manage my image. I'm beginning to realize I don't have to be the master of ceremonies, be talkative, winsome."

Over the next few months, Evan saw more instances of how his striving to impress others could lead to problems when the truth became known. And he began to experiment with being more direct about challenges he had not yet solved, enlisting the help of others.

Writing his Personal Action Plan, his goal became "I will be more self-aware and lead truthfully in a way that relies little on a desire for the positive regard of others." And he made the following *adjustments* in his behavior:

- help others to be their best
- rely on others for problem solving
- notice when I am managing my image and dial it back
- be less guarded when I am uncertain or confused
- stop trying to "prove myself" to everyone all the time
- place more value on the love and validation I find at home
- smile less for the sake of pleasing or "winning over" others

As Evan put all this into action, over time his boss began to trust him more. Evan would make himself vulnerable and acknowledge when he didn't know the answer or when he needed help. And his colleagues were more ready to welcome and support him as a teammate.

He wrote me an email about nine months after the conclusion of our coaching engagement. It began, "You know, I think we changed (adjusted?) my life course in many positive ways." He went on to give me an update on his latest endeavors. And then he closed with this line: "Happy and living my truths!"

PAUL, THE BULLY

Paul was president and CEO of a company founded by his father. Like many leaders I coach, he had already experienced a great deal of success before I came along. Introduced through a mutual friend, I was curious as to why Paul was interested in having a coach.

What I soon learned was that Paul didn't just lead his company of over one hundred employees. He *was* the company. He was a force of nature. And the success of the company depended entirely on him because he was involved in the details of everything. And now he was finally reaching the point where this was no longer sustainable. He used the word "workaholic" at least a half-dozen times in our introductory conversation.

As I introduced the four-dimensional framework to Paul, he quickly realized that "hard work" was his *autopilot*—with both words equally emphasized! Paul didn't just work hard; he could be a hard man to work for. He could be a bully. In one of our early assessments, his score for the "dominance" behavioral trait topped out at 100 percent.

As the weeks passed in our coaching, Paul tuned in more and more to his *emotional* dimension, particularly noticing how often he felt frustration, anger, and bitterness. Bitterness! That is an emotion that often points toward the past. As we sat together one day, I asked Paul to explore the basis for his bitterness more.

He began to tell me about his dad, a hard man himself. When Paul was growing up, his dad never had a good word to say to anyone. No matter what Paul did, he couldn't earn his dad's praise. Paul began to work hard at a young age himself, imitating his father and wanting to please him. But to no avail. One day, when his dad was particularly angry, he said these words to Paul, his sisters, and his brother: "I hope none of you ever has any kids." Those words were seared into Paul's memory.

Think about the message you would take away if you were to hear that message from your father. Indeed, though each of them married, Paul and his sisters never had any kids of their own.

After college, Paul began a successful career working for a large company, opening and running stores for them across the country. One day, in his late thirties, Paul received a phone call from his dad, asking Paul and his wife to move back and help him with the family business. Paul had to be persuaded but finally relented. Once again, he was hoping this might be the opportunity to finally please his dad.

Not long after beginning work with his dad, Paul realized nothing had changed—his dad was still as hard and critical as ever. At the same time, Paul realized the company wasn't doing as well as his father had led him to believe. So as he was used to doing, Paul threw himself into the job, vowing to do "whatever it takes" to win and be successful. His father passed away without Paul ever having heard he had done a good job. Hence, the bitterness and the autopilot mode of nonstop work.

With greater awareness from our coaching sessions, Paul began to notice his emotions more. But instead of letting emotions like frustration or anger control him, he learned to *assess* and *adjust* in the moment and channel these feelings into more constructive interactions with his people.

We did a culture survey of his company, which identified empowerment and team orientation as two areas that needed the most improvement—no big surprise since everything had revolved around and involved Paul up to that point.

Paul's action plan for his own transformation focused on better development of and delegation to his team so that he wasn't always at the center of things. This *adjustment* took time and was risky for Paul. It struck at his core *spiritual* identity, which was up to that point that of a "hard worker." Making himself step back and trust others at times felt like weakness. But gradually, Paul learned to delegate *and* verify that others were getting the work done. Eventually, he made some big hires and brought in experienced outside executives to whom he would entrust key parts of the business.

As time passed, the company no longer had all of its identity wrapped up in Paul, and vice versa. It was able to perform without Paul being the only key performer. As a result of seeing the business could be sustainable whether or not Paul was there to run it, outside investors began to show an interest in acquiring the company. Eventually, Paul sold it for about $50 million. And he began to enjoy a lifestyle where most of his "hard work" was found on the golf course. He had shed the autopilot drivers of bitterness, anger, and the need to prove his worth through hard work. Today I would characterize Paul as a kind and generous man.

CLOSING THOUGHTS AND NEXT STEPS

There you have three stories of leaders who were already leading well but got better. They built on the strengths that had propelled them in leadership while taming the corresponding weaknesses that had sabotaged those strengths. They learned to better lead themselves from within instead of reacting to their external environment or autopilot tendencies.

The process for all of them took time—real change does. And it took the humility and honesty to look at themselves as they never had before. I have written this book with the hope that leaders like you could begin the same honest appraisal in order to get better.

Before I close, I want to emphasize the benefits of considering the help of a professional coach if you really want to grow.[45] You would expect me to say this, since I am a coach and help lead the McKinnon Leadership Group, a boutique coaching company.

But objectively, as I think about what it takes for a leader to change based on nearly fifteen years of observing change in leaders up close, there is no better person who can partner with you than a qualified professional coach. Your boss may want you to grow, but there is no way you would be honest and vulnerable with your boss in the ways needed for real change. You might feel safe with your spouse or best friend, and he or she would encourage you, but he or she is likely not as equipped to help you as a coach would be.

A coach creates a safe, confidential working environment; equips you with tools like the four-dimensional framework I provided you with in this book; is objective in helping you see things as they really are; brings curious questions you would not think to ask yourself; and generally supports you as you take the risks associated with change. A leader-coach partnership is a very special relationship—one that can yield life-changing results.

And now I must close with a question intended to move you ahead:

**What are you going to do next
to lead like you were meant to?**

As you put the suggestions in this book into practice, I'd love to hear how you're doing. Contact me at rob@LeadLikeYou Book.com. And remember to visit LeadLikeYouBook.com for additional resources.

NOTES

1   Ideally, you do this in partnership with a professional
    leadership coach.
2   Executive coach Marshall Goldsmith titled his book using this
    phrase (rev. ed.; New York: Hachette Books, 2007).
3   US Army, Army Field Manual FM 232-100: *The U.S. Army
    Leadership Field Manual* (Stillwell, KS: Digireads.com Publish-
    ing, 2007).
4   *Gladiator*, directed by Ridley Scott (2000, Glendale, CA:
    DreamWorks Pictures).
5   "Heaven"; in Roman mythology, this was the home for heroes
    after death.
6   Bethany Biron, "Fitness Has Exploded into a Nearly $100
    Billion Global Industry as More People Become Obsessed with
    Their Health," *Business Insider*, September 3, 2019, https://
    www.businessinsider.com/fitness-has-exploded-into-a-near-
    ly-100-billion-global-industry-2019-9.
7   Maryann Karinch, *Diets Designed for Athletes* (Champaign, IL:
    Human Kinetics, 2002), viii.
8   "Obesity and Overweight," National Center for Health Sta-
    tistics, US Centers for Disease Control and Prevention, last
    modified June 13, 2016, https://www.cdc.gov/nchs/fastats/obe-
    sity-overweight.htm.
9   Daniel J. Siegel, *Mindsight: The New Science of Personal Trans-
    formation*, Kindle ed. (New York: Random House Publishing
    Group, 2009), 86.

10 David Rock, *Your Brain at Work: Strategies for Overcoming Distraction, Regaining Focus, and Working Smarter All Day Long*, Kindle ed. (New York: HarperCollins, 2009), loc. 236. Inhibiting is the process of not paying attention to something that could be a distraction to the things you do want to pay attention to, which is important when trying to focus on something.

11 Rock, Your Brain at Work, loc. 2013; per Rock, according to Dr. Bruce Lipton, author of *The Biology of Belief*, our conscious brain can pay attention to only around forty environmental cues at one time.

12 Rock, *Your Brain at Work*, p. 121; per Rock, Dr. Bruce Lipton also says our subconscious can pay attention to more than two million environmental cues at one time.

13 "Coaching and the Brain," *Choice Magazine*, September 2009.

14 "Certainty creates a reward response in the brain that enables healthy PFC [prefrontal cortex] functionality. Too much ambiguity, change and risk makes us uncomfortable and sets off our primitive alarm bells, producing what we call a threatened brain state. Such conditions shut down PFC functionality." *Choice Magazine*, 30–31.

15 "Something else we know about the brain is that we think in maps, and we use many parts of the brain all connected together, for even relatively simple thinking processes. The neural pathways that make up these mental maps become stronger and more embedded the more we use them. This means the more we hold particular mental maps in mind, the easier it is for the brain to continue using those maps. . . . The more we focus on problems, the more we embed the neural pathways associated with problems. Taking a solutions approach . . . helps others to create new mental maps, as opposed to further embedding . . . maps associated with problems." *Choice Magazine*, 31.

16 Rock, *Your Brain at Work*, 224.

17 John B. Arden, *Rewire Your Brain: Think Your Way to a Better Life* (Hoboken, NJ: John Wiley & Sons, 2010), 6. Your brain

contains a hundred billion neurons, and each of these neurons is able to maintain connections with about ten thousand other neurons.

18 As in the intellectual domain, neuroscience has revealed a lot about the brain's role in originating and controlling our emotions. I use the "heart" as the traditional metaphorical repository of our feelings.

19 The Corporate Executive Board, in a 2004 study on employee engagement, surveyed fifty thousand employees at fifty-nine global companies. The study concluded that emotional factors were four times more effective at engaging employees than rational factors. Leigh Buchanan, "The Things They Do For Love," *Harvard Business Review*, December 2004.

20 Richard Rohr, *Immortal Diamond: Searching for Our True Self* (San Francisco: Jossey-Bass, 2013).

21 This is not meant to be an all-inclusive list of recognized religions. Also, in this context, I define "religion" broadly as living (or trying to live) according to a set of beliefs and practices considered meaningful. Such beliefs and practices can be based on formally documented doctrine (organized religion) or established cultural practices (folk religion).

22 Dictionary.com, s.v. "authentic," accessed March 22, 2020, https://www.dictionary.com/browse/authentic.

23 Dallas Willard, "Willard Words," http://old.dwillard.org/resources/WillardWords.asp.

24 US Senator John McCain delivered remarks on the occasion of Veterans Day at the McConnell Center, University of Louisville, Kentucky, on November 11, 2009.

25 Parker J. Palmer, *Let Your Life Speak: Listening for the Voice of Vocation*, Kindle ed. (San Francisco: Jossey-Bass, 2009), loc. 78.

26 S. M. Schaefer et al., "Purpose in Life Predicts Better Emotional Recovery from Negative Stimuli," *PLOS ONE* 8, no. 11 (2013).

27 Gladwell, Malcolm, *Outliers: The Story of Success* (New York: Little, Brown and Company, 2008), 40.

28 Deut. 6:4–5 (New King James Version).

29 Mark 12:30 (NKJV).

30 Alexander Caillet, "The Thinking Path," Corentus, accessed March 24, 2020, https://corentus.com/the-thinking-path.

31 The spiritual dimension, as we have learned, is unique from the other three. It is a constant, regardless of our default dimension.

32 If you are familiar with the Enneagram framework, you might recognize a lot of similarity here with the three triads: heart (numbers 2, 3, and 4), head (numbers 5, 6, and 7), and gut (numbers 8, 9, and 1). My leaders find the Enneagram to be a very helpful assessment for self-awareness and better knowing themselves.

33 Often through formative experiences while growing up.

34 Think Andy Grove, former CEO of Intel. He turned his maxim "Only the paranoid survive" into a classic book on leadership in the 1990s.

35 Again, this generally is formed through experiences in their upbringing.

36 As a head person myself, I continue to work on this. My wife would tell you that I can be midsentence replying to her in a conversation, and suddenly I pause for an inordinate amount of time—I have suddenly had a new thought that I am processing. This thought takes me somewhere else, away from being present in the conversation with Marta!

37 Navy Lieutenant Mike Murphy provides an especially dramatic example of this, as depicted in the book and movie *Lone Survivor*. The four-man Seal team that he led was outnumbered, pinned down in enemy territory, and unable to reach headquarters with their radio. In a heroic act of self-sacrifice for his team members, Murphy walked out to open ground to get a cell signal and call for help, fully exposed to enemy fire and certain death. He and two other Seals perished that day, but Petty Officer Marcus Luttrell survived to tell the story. Marcus Luttrell and Patrick Robinson, *Lone Survivor: The Eyewitness Account of*

Operation Redwing and the Lost Heroes of SEAL Team 10 (New York: Little, Brown and Company, 2007).

38 One such book that comes to mind, though not widely available, is Michael M. Lobardo and Robert W. Eichinger's *For Your Improvement*, 4th ed. (Minneapolis: Lominger Limited, 2004).

39 Remember, it took years to become this way in the first place!

40 Alan Morinis in *Everyday Holiness: The Jewish Spiritual Path of Mussar*, writes:

> "If you've lost your job but still have your family and health, you have something to be grateful for.
>
> If you can't move around except in a wheelchair but your mind is as sharp as ever, you have something to be grateful for.
>
> If your house burns down but you still have your memories, you have something to be grateful for.
>
> If you've broken a string on your violin and you still have three more, you have something to be grateful for."

(Boston: Trumpeter Books, 2011), 64.

41 Prov. 17:22 (NKJV).

42 Prov. 23:7 (NKJV) (paraphrase).

43 Jocko Willink and Leif Babin, *Extreme Ownership: How U.S. Navy Seals Lead and Win* (New York: St. Martin's Press, 2015).

44 Or longer, as necessary, until you have accomplished the degree of transformation you want.

45 A professional coach (as distinguished from someone who calls themselves a coach) is a member of an established organization such as the International Coaching Federation (www.coachfederation.org), has received instruction and passed a curriculum of best practices in coach training, and adheres to a professional code of ethics.

ACKNOWLEDGMENTS

My first word of thanks goes to all the leaders who, over the past fifteen years, have invited me to come alongside them, opened their lives to me, and allowed me a front-row seat to witness how they learn to lead from the best versions of who they are. I wish I could name you all individually, but you know who you are.

Second, I wish to thank two men in particular who have coached me and been instrumental in helping me become who I was meant to be—Jerry Leachman and Trip Sizemore. You two know the "before" and "after," but most importantly, you helped me travel the "in-between."

I am also grateful for my late brother, Don, who was my first hero and taught me the fundamentals of navigating life and business. He would be very interested in and supporting this work the whole way.

A special thank-you goes to Georgetown coaching teacher Lloyd Raines who, when I first said to him, "I have nothing new to say," replied with, "But Rob, when it is spoken in your voice, it all becomes new."

I began writing this book in 2009. My friends have grown tired of asking me when it would be done. Nevertheless, I appreciate their good-natured encouragement over the decade, especially that of Hunter Bates, John Lynch, Claudius Modesti, Dan Polk, Noah Riner, and Yasser Youssef.

Among my friends, I am so grateful that one chose to come alongside me and cofound The McKinnon Leadership Group. Brad Sytsma has been and is a daily "upper" for so much of this journey. Along with Brad, I am also indebted to Clay Parcells, who was the first to embrace The McKinnon Way of leadership coaching, and has been a steadfast collaborator ever since.

Thank you to Amanda Rooker, who helped me move from notes to book plan to first draft. Her wise guidance did a lot to shape this book. And thank you to the crew at Girl Friday Productions in Seattle, who helped turn it into a finished product.

I am so thankful for supportive parents-in-law, Bob and Janneke, who, along with Marta, patiently read every draft and provided constructive feedback.

And thanks to my incredible and wise kids, Ellie and Will, who were there at the very beginning and have enthusiastically supported this work all the way through to selection of the book cover. Your encouragement has meant so much to me.

Finally, Marta. Pastor Tim Keller says that the purpose of marriage is to shape you into the person God made you to be. For over thirty years, Marta has been fulfilling her role in helping me be a better husband, dad, friend, and coach. I could not write enough pages to thank her for all she means to me.

ABOUT THE AUTHOR

Rob McKinnon writes and speaks on leadership, and has coached CEOs and their executive teams for over fifteen years. He is passionate about helping leaders lead well.

Leaders who have worked with Rob report that the insights they gain and personal transformation they are able to make are like no other leadership development program they have ever experienced.

Rob trains other coaches in his "McKinnon Way of Leadership Coaching" methodology. And he is co-founder of The McKinnon Leadership Group, a boutique coaching firm that caters to CEOs, senior executives and leadership teams.

After graduating with a business degree from Wheaton College, Rob served four years as an Army Armor officer, leading combat-ready forces in Europe. He earned an MBA from the Robert H. Smith School of Business, University of Maryland, and completed postgraduate studies in leadership coaching at Georgetown University in Washington, DC. Rob holds the Master Certified Coach designation with the International Coaching Federation.

Rob lives with his wife, Marta, just outside Charlottesville, Virginia.

To learn more about Rob and sign up for his occasional leadership blog posts, please visit www.robmckinnon.com.

ADDITIONAL RESOURCES

Keynote. Rob's keynote on "Lead Like You Were Meant To" comes with a guarantee: you will leave the room a better leader than when you walked in. (Available in-person and virtually.) *Please visit robmckinnon.com/speaking.*

Workshop. Jump in for an immersive experience of "Lead Like You Were Meant To" that enables leaders to bring their real-world challenges into the classroom and develop new strategies for leading out of a better version of themselves. (Available in-person and virtually.) *Please visit robmckinnon. com/speaking.*

Leadership Coaching. If you want to grow further as a leader, partner with one of the experienced coaches at The McKinnon Leadership Group. Our methodology helps you know yourself better than ever before, so that you can lead out of the best version of yourself – lead like you were meant to! *Please visit mckinnonleadershipgroup.com.*

Leadership Team Coaching & Retreats. If your executive leadership team is a great collection of individuals, but not reaching its potential as a high-performance team, Rob can help. He'll coach you through conversations you've never had before, leading to breakthroughs in building trust and functioning as the team you were meant to be. *Please visit robmckinnon.com.*

Coach Training. Are you great at having coaching conversations, but lack a comprehensive coaching framework for your leaders? The McKinnon Way is a proven methodology that consistently helps leaders experience tangible, lasting change in themselves. *Please visit robmckinnon.com/coach-training.*

Podcast. Join the "Five O'Clock Leadership" conversation with Brad and Rob as they share their latest learning from leaders about leadership. Fun, witty and current, this podcast offers fresh perspectives on how to lead with your best self. *Search for "Five O'Clock Leadership" wherever you listen to podcasts, or visit mckinnonleadershipgroup.com/podcast to listen today.*

Book Resources. Continue to grow into the leader you were meant to be with additional self-development exercises, author videos and more. *Please visit LeadLikeYouBook.com or robmckinnon.com/book.*

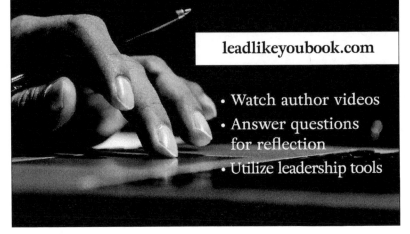